Developing and Administering
a Comprehensive
High School Music Program

Developing
and Administering
a Comprehensive
High School Music Program

HARRY E. MOSES

PARKER PUBLISHING COMPANY, INC.
West Nyack, N.Y.

© 1970 BY

PARKER PUBLISHING COMPANY, INC.

WEST NYACK, N.Y.

LIBRARY OF CONGRESS
CATALOG CARD NUMBER: 78–121709

PRINTED IN THE UNITED STATES OF AMERICA
ISBN 0–13–204156–1
B&P

To
Ruth

For her dedication and help in preparing the manuscript of this book

What You Can Expect
from This Book

Our times call for music educators with broad perspectives. Singing songs, playing instruments and leading a choir and band are only some of the activities which make up the music program. There must be a completely integrated program with all the offerings related to each other and with the entire curriculum growing out of a broad educational plan. For 50 years music educators have been advocating a program of music for everyone. This book shows how it can be done successfully.

Outlined here is a complete and meaningful curriculum, one in which a variety of courses is offered, all interrelated and growing out of the General Music Course which serves as its base. The music program which it advocates puts the specialties such as the choir and band in proper perspective, each as a part of the larger educational plan. In order to identify with the general curriculum, the program should be set up to meet the needs of all of the students.

A diversity of vocal and instrumental courses, listening activities, creative music classes, special assemblies, music clubs, in- and out-of-school concert attendance, all are surely part of the curriculum. For those who wish to specialize, there should be a variety of musical experiences available. For those who aspire to become competent musical amateurs—both performers and listeners—there should also be a number of courses from which to choose. This book shows how all of these musical activities are interrelated and together make up the coordinated music program.

I will discuss how administrators can unleash talents for planning by teachers and students in order to evolve a realistic and workable curriculum, and how superintendents, directors and supervisors can set up educational and administrative procedures to help the teacher function effectively and thereby improve instruction. Before students can be "turned on," I feel that it is important that administrators and teachers be fully and enthusiastically involved in the music program.

In the preparation of school budgets, the expansion of the music department must be justified. A comprehensive program, one which reaches all of the students, is more attractive than a limited one. The curriculum outlined in this book will be of interest to those who manage the educational affairs and those whose function it is to approach the school board for funds.

There is a great need for and interest in the general music approach as outlined here. The number of requests from teachers, supervisors and administrators as a result of my articles in professional periodicals indicates that a broad curriculum which grows out of the general music course has meaning for educators. In this book I will draw on my experience as a teacher, and music educator, and chairman of the music department in a senior high school. Practical solutions to the everyday problems met in high schools are suggested. The book can be used by anyone actively engaged in the field of music education.

Harry E. Moses

Contents

What You Can Expect from This Book • 7

One—Facing the Problems of the High School Music Program • 19

Relating Music to the General Curriculum • Demonstrating and Teaching New Skills • Developing Teacher Flexibility and Versatility • Overcoming Conflicts in the Schedule • Overcoming Conflicts Between the Arts and the Sciences • Integrating the General Music Program into the Curriculum of General Education • Teaching General Music in Depth • Using General Music to Stimulate Interest in the Specialties • Developing an Academic-Music Curriculum • Encouraging Students to Become Competent Amateurs • Distributing the Workload Among Teachers • Avoiding Overlapping and Duplication in the Schedule • Enlisting Community Support • Financing the Music Program • Planning Support for a Program Which Meets Larger Needs

Two—Basing the Program on the General Music Course • 27

Broadening the Approach Through a Link with the Curriculum in General Education • Defining the Curriculum • Defining the Function of the General Music Course • Organizing an Interrelated Music Curriculum • Determining the Basis for Developing a General Music Course • Utiliz-

Two—Basing the Program on the General Music Course (*cont.*)

ing Teacher Skills ● Developing Student Interest and Skill ● Listing the Functions of the General Music Course ● Recruiting for the Specialties in the General Music Course ● Utilizing a Wide Variety of Musical Experiences ● Contrasting the Logical and Psychological Approaches ● Presenting Several Approaches to the General Music Course ● Using Popular, Folk, and Ethnic Music ● Arranging a Balanced Content in the General Music Course ● Encouraging Students to Explore in Music ● Utilizing the World Scene and Daily Living as a Setting for a Course of Study ● Using the Language of Music as a Means of Communication ● Using Note-Reading as One Type of Musical Experience ● Teaching Students to Evaluate Their Musical Experiences ● Meeting Musical Needs Through a General Music Course

Three—Developing the Vocal Music Program ● 39

Capitalizing on the Universality of Singing ● Channeling Potential Singers into a Vocal Program ● Knowing and Understanding the Adolescent Voice ● Planning for a Wide and Balanced Vocal Program ● Placing the Choir and Other Vocal Specialty Groups in Proper Perspective ● Teaching a Choir How to Acquire a Beautiful Tone ● Using Tone Blending ● Teaching Music Reading for Part Singing ● Making Music from the Beginning ● Planning the Seating and Standing Arrangements ● Facing Rehearsal Problems ● Placing the Emphasis on the Music ● Conducting the Rehearsal ● Developing Built-In Disciplines ● Organizing the Practice Period ● Developing Morale in a Singing Group ● Involving Choir Members in Organizational Problems ● Developing a Choral and Vocal Library ● Building a Repertory of Choral Compositions ● Initiating Unskilled Singers in Choral Groups ● Relating the Choir Program to the Curriculum in General Education ● Preparing a Vocal Program Which Meets the Needs of All of the Students ● Organizing Voice Classes ● Building a Repertory for Voice Students ● Supervising Voice Training and Practice ● Overtaxing the Voice ● Scheduling Advanced Vocal Training for Gifted Pupils ● Using Music Written for the Theatre ● Developing Small Vocal Ensembles ● Using Folk and Popular Music ● Involving a Large Number of Students in a Singing Activity ● Building Morale, Character and a Cultural Life

Four—Developing the Instrumental Music Program ● 57

Positive Aspects of the Instrumental Program ● Lag Between Philosophy and Practice ● When to Begin Instrumental Instruction ● Class Instruction ● Necessity for Proper Facilities ● Importance of Ensemble Playing ● Motivations for Playing an Instrument ● Technics, Materials, and Courses of Study ● Scheduling Instrumental Classes ● Courses of Study ● The Development of the Marching Band ● The Band and Community

Four—Developing the Instrumental Music Program (*cont.*)

Relations ● The Marching Band and the Concert Band ● Selecting Literature for the Concert Band ● Conducting the Band Rehearsal ● Seating Charts for Bands of Various Sizes ● Formation for a Marching Band of Eighty Players ● Encouraging the Musical Growth of the Band ● Organizing the School Orchestra ● Recruiting for the School Orchestra ● Building an Interest in Playing Stringed Instruments ● Making a Start with the High School Orchestra ● The Wide and Varied Background of the Conductor ● The Development of a Singing Tone in the Orchestra ● Aptitude and Coordination for Playing an Instrument ● Choosing and Keeping an Instrument in Proper Playing Condition ● The Importance of Developing Good Intonation ● Balance and Intonation ● The Concertmaster and First Chair Positions ● Seating Plans for Orchestras of Various Sizes ● Handling Discipline Problems ● Planning Musical Programs ● Popular Music in the Instrumental Program

Five—Stimulating Musicianship ● 85

What Is Musicianship? ● Who Can Become Musical? ● Implications for the Music Curriculum ● Basic Responses to Music ● Musicianship Comes from Studying the Music ● Creative Music Classes ● Dividing the Class into Working Units ● Setting Up a Rotating System for Unit Teaching ● Programming Units of Work ● Hearing the Music ● Modern Trends in Harmony ● Relevance and Function of Creative Work ● Electing a Creative Music Course

Six—Teaching Music Appreciation and Music Literature ● 97

Meaning, Relevance and Identification ● Understanding What Makes a Piece of Music Great ● Music, Emotions, and Communications ● Two Approaches to Appreciation ● Popular and Folk Music ● Organizing for the Teaching of Subject Matter ● The Emotional Approach ● The Intellectual Approach ● The Developmental Approach ● Utilizing the Concerns of Youth ● Concerns with War in Music ● Concern with Boy-Girl Relationships in Music ● Music and the Generation Gap ● Music, Social Problems, and Politics ● Music and Identification ● Technical Music Materials ● Preparing a Course of Study ● The Teaching of Music Literature ● Modern to Classical Approach ● Who Should Elect the Course ● The Psychological Approach ● Materials and Equipment ● Other Listening Opportunities ● Developing a Lending Record Library

Seven—Placing Music in the Overall Curriculum ● 115

Using Music for Motivation ● Music and the Organic Curriculum ● Utilizing the Music Teacher as a Resource Person ● Scheduling Resource Teachers ● Integrating Music and Science Teaching ● Studying Music as a Science ● Studying Music as an Art ● Relating Music and History

Seven—Placing Music in the Overall Curriculum (*cont.*)

• Viewing Music as a Social Art • Evolving Forms and Styles Reflect a Changing Society • Relating Music and Foreign Languages • Relating Music and English Literature • Understanding the Difference Between a Play and an Opera—*Othello* and *Otello* • Relating Music and Grammar • Teaching Music and Art • Combining Music and the Dance • Motivating Interest Through an Organic Curriculum

Eight—Organizing Effective Assembly Programs • 133

Functions of Music in the Assembly • Organizing the Committee • Allotting Time for the Assemblies • The Assemblies and General Education • Listening Versus Active Participation • The Community Sing • Song Materials • Technics for Improving the Tone • Using Religious Music • Radio and TV Technics • Leading Community Singing • Part Singing in the Assembly • Preparing Other Types of Programs • Preparing the Musical Quiz • Using Musical Films • Utilization of Student Talent • Using Alumni Talent • Planning Concert and Festival Programs

Nine—Performing in Concerts, Festivals, and Contests • 153

Organizing for Mass Education and Mass Activity • Benefiting from Mass Activity • Organizing Student Committees • Performing in School • Performing in the Community • Working for Broader Objectives • Relating Concerts to Musical Growth • Motivation for Educational and Emotional Growth • Seating Large Numbers of Performers • The Music Festival • Group Participation • Opera Workshop Presentation • Operetta and Musical Comedy • Musical Revue and Variety Show • Cantata and Oratorio Performances • Musical Contests

Ten—Scheduling and Giving Credit for Music Subjects • 167

Basic Purposes of a Music Schedule • Scheduling Based on Need • Scheduling Based on Teacher Flexibility • Scheduling for the Many • Scheduling and the Length of the School Day • Scheduling in the Large High School • Scheduling the Homeroom and the Assembly • Scheduling in the Small High School • Scheduling and the Computer • Computer Help for an Integrated Curriculum • Scheduling for the Talented Student • Scheduling for the Handicapped Child • Scheduling for the Disadvantaged Student • Scheduling for Practice Rooms • Earning Carnegie Units • Scheduling Activities for Little or No Credit • Devising Other Motivations • Granting Honor Points

Eleven—Developing the Music Teacher • 183

Choosing the Teacher • Developing Teacher Philosophy and Goals • Developing a Positive Personality • Developing Relationships with Students • Setting Up Classroom Procedures and Disciplines • Preparing

Eleven—Developing the Music Teacher (*cont.*)

Seating Plans ● Directions for Using Seating Chart Cards ● Assigning Homework ● Developing Teacher Communication ● Developing Resourcefulness ● Developing Relationships with Administrators ● Developing Relationships with Parents and the Community ● Joining Professional Organizations ● Developing Teacher Morale

Twelve—Evaluating and Organizing Facilities, Equipment, and Materials ● 197

Involving Music Teachers in the Planning ● Using Source Materials and References ● Building All-Purpose Rooms ● Planning the Auditorium ● Locating the Music Department Quarters ● Planning the Size of Classrooms ● Setting the Ceiling Level ● Planning for Proper Lighting ● Planning the Choral Room ● Using a Flexible Seating Plan ● Providing Musical Equipment ● Planning the Orchestral and Band Room ● Planning the Practice Rooms ● Planning Facilities for a Small Music Department ● Preparing the General Music Classroom ● Planning the Music Department Office ● Storing Music and Books ● Planning Storage Space ● Building the Music Department Library

Index ● 217

Developing and Administering a Comprehensive High School Music Program

One

Facing the Problems
of the High School
Music Program

Relating Music to the General Curriculum

      The high school music teacher is faced with a number of problems for which he must find solutions. He must concern himself with the school in a changing world and with the immediate problems of the school in the community. Continual adjustments are necessary in evolving a program which is based on the everyday struggle with the concerns of youth. Skills that are needed today must be taught in such a way that students are prepared for the opportunities of tomorrow. If the teacher accepts the general music approach to the curriculum, his first thoughts will be with bringing music to ever larger groups of students.

  There are sociological problems which must be considered in the formulation of any educational program. Mobility of population, diversity of ethnic and racial groups, loss of identity because of the great numbers of students in schools, and general restlessness all have serious implications for the educator. New approaches, methods, and materials that are meaningful to students in a rapidly changing society must be found.

Demonstrating and Teaching New Skills

Teachers should accept the fact that in order to keep up with a changing society it is necessary periodically to learn new skills. Somewhere along the line, as the program grows, it becomes desirable for the teachers to demonstrate and teach new skills. It may very well be that the vocal music teacher will find it necessary to play the guitar in order to accompany a class in the singing of folk songs and ballads. The instrumental teacher may find that some training is required for "bandstrating" an arrangement for a small combo. A theory and harmony teacher may need to add to his background a knowledge of serial and electronic music. Acquiring new skills as they are needed will broaden the teacher's background.

Young people, today, have a great respect for instructors who are aware of what is current in the field. When the teacher reveals a knowledge of popular music, superior to that of the students, greater confidence for learning is established. It is not difficult, then, to convince students that there is much to learn in the field of popular music that is admirable— and that there is much that is insignificant. Music teachers work in the realm of good taste and discrimination. Why not teach judgment values in the field of popular music? This is an area where students can be helped to resolve existing conflicts.

Developing Teacher Flexibility and Versatility

The highly specialized teacher is an asset, not a liability. He brings to the music curriculum special skills which are needed and through which he can build technically good performance groups. The tendency, however, will be for these teachers to work only in the specialties. In public school music it is desirable that teachers be more flexible and more versatile. This versatility need not mean a watering down of teacher skills, but can lead to the broadening of his musicianship and his outlook on educational goals. Good teachers, therefore, should work towards broadening their skills as a basis for expanding the curriculum.

The highly specialized music teacher must also be acquainted with all of the gadgets and trappings available for classroom use—the FM Multiplex radio, television (closed circuit and otherwise), the tape recorder, the stereo record player, the computer with its new potential for testing students or making a new kind of music. These testify to how far we have come. The modern teacher can choose to ignore it all, or elect to use the devices to make music courses more meaningful.

Overcoming Conflicts in the Schedule

The conflict between academic and music subjects for time in the schedule creates an additional problem. Both are important; each meets a different need. The origin of the problem dates back to the development of the Sputnik. At that time, the shattered free world rushed to the schools to create a rigid scientific and mathematical system which would not only match the achievements of the Russians, but would out-distance them. Within a very short period of time most of the educational institutions in the United States and the free world were pursuing a course designed for the mass production of scientists, mathematicians and engineers. The humanities were relegated to an unimportant position in the educational scheme. Music and art now began to appear on the fringe of the roster. Where previously students had a free choice of electives, it was suddenly found that their rosters were filled with science and mathematics. Music courses, in some places, began to appear as one- and two-period minors and were offered before school or after school, or not at all. The orchestra, the band and the choir, the privileged groups, suffered a similar fate. Formerly featured as a part of the regular schedule, they now came into conflict with new requirements. The courses were pushed to the outer extremities of the roster. It seemed as if 50 years of progress in the field of music education were about to be wiped out.

In many places, music education is still at this point. To some extent, the roster has become flexible again, but music still must fight for its place in the overall curriculum. Students who are planning for a career in mathematics or science still have little room in their programs for an elective music course. Those who choose a career in music also find that college entrance requirements necessitate a wide battery of academic subjects which are required for college entrance, thus limiting the number of music courses which they can elect. Administrators have now come to see that this was a mistake and are trying to correct the situation. Our world needs mathematicians, scientists, and engineers who are educated in the humanities. A number of leading technical institutions and colleges now recognize that the exclusion of the humanities has produced graduates of limited vision. They are now in the process of initiating a broad program of the arts where none heretofore existed. If the administrators in the high school also believe in a balanced program of general education, they too can resolve the conflict which relegated the humanities to a secondary position.

Overcoming Conflicts Between the Arts and the Sciences

Music teachers have been helping to bring a complete change in emphasis. Leaders in this field were quick to see the fallacy of an all scientific world and spoke out against it. The Music Educators National Conference ardently took up the battle on behalf of the humanities. Music directors and individual teachers inaugurated special campaigns to point out the harm which could result from a plan which limits the arts in our general educational program. Once again, music is slowly being placed in proper perspective as an integral part of the complete program of the school. The task must be completed and the music curriculum expanded, and music educators must see that it is not minimized again. One of the best ways of doing this is to set up a plan in which music is available for all students in the high school. No one would recommend eliminating a healthy, growing business.

Integrating the General Music Program into the Curriculum in General Education

How can we hope to bring about this desirable change in music education? One way, of course, is to set up the General Music Course as the base for the whole music curriculum. Another is to integrate music with a whole battery of academic subjects so that it enhances what is already accepted in the curriculum. This may mean that while some of the specialties will remain on the fringe of the roster, the General Music Course will move into the regular schedule as a base from which the whole curriculum can grow. If we establish an overall plan, one designed to meet the needs of all of the students, administrators are more likely to be sympathetic. The greater the number of students involved, the more support the program will receive, but the music teachers must take the initiative. Without their willingness to build such a program, this approach cannot be established in the curriculum.

Teaching General Music in Depth

Once the general music approach is accepted in the overall schedule, it is the responsibility of the music educators to see that it is taught in depth. If we are to make the course meaningful, it must relate itself to life and the interests and concerns of young people. Here, it is not important that large areas of materials be covered. It is more important that the quality of the teaching insures a broad, cultural background for the pupils, one on which they can draw and build for the remainder of their lives. The General Music Course, as we shall see, has unlimited sources upon which to draw. The teacher who capitalizes on these helps to pave the way for an ever broadening program.

The General Music Course can also help to bring prestige to the larger curriculum. If we are attempting to reach all of the students in the school, the sheer size of the program will give it status and importance. It is not the size in itself that is important; it is the fact that we try to bring music to more people that is significant. Implicit in the whole concept of general education is some standard of quality. Any plans which are made to bring music to larger groups of students must take into consideration educational outcomes which are meaningful. Summarizing, we can state that a program in depth can lead novices in music to a large number of desirable outcomes, one of which may be the choice of a specialty.

Using General Music to Stimulate Interest in the Specialties

As the general music program unfolds, arrangements can be made for the small, talented group of students to reveal itself and indicate a need for greater specialization. These groups which will appear will determine which of the specialties are needed in the curriculum. As they become a part of the larger program, they also become a part of the complete and interrelated schedule of activities which the general music approach advocates. The attempt to reach all of the students in the school can also lead to better communications with parents and the community. Thus, also, related problems, such as those dealing with the conflict between music and academic subjects in the roster, can be resolved in the best interests of providing a balanced educational program.

Developing an Academic-Music Curriculum

There is another advantage: that is the emergence of the academic-music curriculum. This college preparatory course is designed to meet the needs of high specialization. Students who aim to become teachers and performers should be encouraged to elect it. Many students, however, are not certain at the beginning of high school about music as a profession or vocation. The academic-music curriculum allows them to take a full range of academic subjects and elect needed music courses which could be used later for college entrance requirements.

Encouraging Students to Become Competent Amateurs

Ideally, music teachers should aim to make a musician of everyone, the professional and the layman. Practically, they prepare the most precocious students to rise to the top of the profession and encourage all of the others to use the arts for enrichment. Teachers are careful not to encourage potential amateurs to specialize at the expense of a broader education. The most talented pupils, of course, should be encouraged to pursue a career; others can be directed to enhance their lives by making or creatively listening to music. Whether they play, sing or listen, there is an opportunity for musical growth in all high school students. The belief in the general music approach is based on this premise.

Distributing the Workload Among Teachers

The workload of the music teachers is directly related to the problems involved in the scheduling of a full roster of musical activities. With the expansion of the program, and the increase in the number of curricular and extracurricular offerings, comes the necessity for more teacher time and more effective distribution of the workload. Teacher skills must be taken into consideration. One teacher may have been engaged, originally, as a choral specialist. Because of a vacancy in the roster, it may seem that he is the logical one to take over the theory and harmony class. If he is poorly qualified in this area, it might seem best to shuffle the teacher rosters in order that students receive the best instruction available. It is desirable, in the selection of teachers, that versatile candidates be chosen to compliment each other. This can then be worked out, in making teacher assignments on the roster, to the satisfaction of everyone. First consideration, however, should be given to the students who must get effective instruction. By utilizing the large variety of skills available on the staff, a wider and broader program can be planned. The workload should be fairly distributed so that each instructor can do an effective job and teacher morale will be maintained.

Avoiding Overlapping and Duplication in the Schedule

Precautions should be taken against duplication of effort. The program should be evaluated periodically, to see if teacher time can be picked up by the elimination of overlapping or duplication. There are additional activities which need implementation. Often teacher time can be used to greater advantage. In any large program there should be room for courses in music appreciation and music literature. These should not duplicate each other, as they sometimes do. In some schools, there are a senior choir, junior choir, vocal ensemble, a girls glee club, a boys glee club and perhaps a mixed glee club. All of these activities require teacher time. Some of these activities, perhaps, can be merged, to find teacher time for other developing interests. For the good of the overall program, it might be best to consolidate a number of these activities in order to make available a more varied number of offerings.

Enlisting Community Support

A major problem for educators is to secure school and community support for a complete music curriculum. Music teachers in the past have had little trouble in securing support for the marching band and the choir. Parent groups, student athletic associations, community service clubs and businessmen's associations can always be depended upon to support the high school performing organizations. There should be more effective ways, however, to support these organizations, as a part of a larger budget for a more complete department of music.

Financing the Music Program

Financing and supporting a full well-rounded program of activities require serious consideration by school boards. Musical instruments, band uniforms, choir robes, music and adequate facilities are expensive. The Music Department as a whole, however, has a product to sell. Its value to the whole scheme of general education is neither greater nor lesser than, let us say, the English or Social Studies Departments. For the most part, wherever music is given, the contribution to the life of the school has been outstanding. As a matter of record, however, music teachers have over-sold the specialties, hoping that the bands and choirs, the display groups, would always speak for the entire curriculum. What has resulted was that teachers became so busy with the specialties, as they grew in size and quality, that they neglected whole areas in music education which were needed in the schools. It is to be hoped that as the music programs expand, with the growth of the general education movement, school boards will finance the larger programs so that all music courses can take their proper place in the curriculum.

The marching band and the a cappella choir need no boost from us. Remarkable strides have been made in both of these areas. When we consider the number of children who benefit from these activities in a school, however, we see a different picture. At the most, a small percentage of the students in a school are involved. If we believe that music is good for people, why not make it available for all of the students? We have been doing very well in music education. New trends show that we can do better.

Planning Support for a Program Which Meets Larger Needs

This, then, becomes a problem for administrators: can we secure more money for additional teachers, better materials and facilities, to meet larger needs; or should we curtail certain aspects of the program in order to give more students an opportunity to elect courses in music which are varied and meet other needs?

There are two approaches to the problem: first, we must look at the existing curriculum to see where and if there is any overscheduling or duplication. Second, we must try to build a well-coordinated, integrated program, which serves the needs of the entire school. Good administrators will help when they are convinced that it is educationally sound to permit the program to expand. Music teachers must make every effort to sell the entire program. It is the ultimate solution to most of their problems.

Music educators can sell this broader program to the school board. The enthusiasm of the teachers for a complete well-balanced curriculum can be contagious. Administrators and the school board must be exposed to the implications of a more balanced series of courses. Communication with and the indoctrination of the school board is imperative. Superintendents and board members may be invited to see demonstrations showing how students in the General Music Course, in instrumental classes are encouraged to participate in all kinds of activities which prepare them for more specialized participation. Hearing a polished band or choir is one thing; witnessing all of the preliminary activities which motivate and prepare students to go on to more advanced courses is a revelation for those who are not aware of what goes into building a broader program.

We have been trying to present some of the difficulties in music education which confront those who are responsible for setting up and administering a program in music education. Possible solutions have been only briefly suggested. In the following chapters we offer more concrete suggestions. Conditions, of course, vary from school to school. Basically, however, our problems are the same, varying only in degree. Teachers have to be aware of conditions which exist and search for answers.

Two

Basing the Program
on the General
Music Course

**Broadening the Approach Through a Link with the
Curriculum in General Education**

In our search for a curriculum to
meet the needs of all of the students, we must refer to the objectives of
the program in general education. True, we have to be realistic enough
to meet budgetary considerations; but we must also be honest enough to
recognize that the time has come to broaden the music schedule of activities. If we throw our lot in with the expansion in general education money
can be found.

It should not be inferred here, that the lack of general music classes
means that a school does not have a good music program. Where there is
an excellent vocal teacher, highly developed programs in community
singing and vocal ensembles are found. Where a school has on its staff
an excellent musicologist, tremendous growth in appreciation and listening classes becomes apparent. The work of creative teachers who develop complete courses around music composition and the making of
primitive instruments is well known. These manifestations of inspired
and exciting teaching all have their place in our schools.

Specialized courses such as these, however, should not be used as a
substitute for the General Music Course. In proper perspective, they can
only be seen as more tails on a wagging dog. The elimination of these

activities is not being advocated. On the contrary, a system is recommended here which will strengthen the highly specialized courses as a part of the larger curriculum. The overall, comprehensive music program, as it finally evolves, should grow out of the general music courses and serve all of the students in our schools.

The new leisure requires that amateurs in music be trained for competency, both in performance and in listening. Participation in amateur symphony orchestras, choirs, chamber music groups and church choirs, requires the learning of basic skills on a high level. Attendance at concert, opera, and recital programs can become enriched musical experiences when the listener is prepared for active listening. The General Music Course can whet the appetite of amateurs for competent participation in music at all levels. Today it is no longer necessary to prove the importance of music in our daily lives. Our problem, now, is: *How can we best bring music to large masses of people in a meaningful way?*

Defining the Curriculum

Before a case can be made for the general music program, we must be able to demonstrate its importance in the more complete picture. The music curriculum is the sum total of experiences to which all of our students are exposed and through which they develop musically. In this curriculum we include all of the regular courses, assemblies, clubs, and all other pursuits which enrich the musical life of the school.

As we look at each musical activity we try to see it, first, as an important part of the larger musical program and second, as part of the entire school program. Each course should be weighed periodically and measured in terms of its function in the complete schedule. It may very well be that we will want both music appreciation and music literature as separate courses. If we do, we should know why, and students who elect one or both should be keenly aware of the difference between the two.

Defining the Function of the General Music Course

When we shift the emphasis in the music curriculum to the General Music Course as the backbone of the program, we can come to a clear understanding of the function of this class. We can define its terms and goals. We can set it up to serve the needs of those students who want to get the most out of music without specializing, and we can also have the course provide a cultural background for those who have elected to specialize.

Figure 2–1 shows the organization of a music curriculum in a large school which employs a number of teachers. We present it as an ideal program towards which all schools can work. Each school should strive to develop and expand the music schedule with the needs as they are revealed.

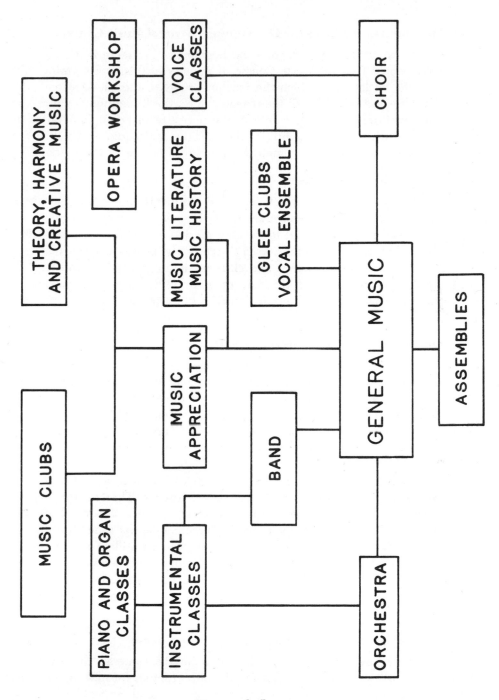

Figure 2–1

Determining the Basis for Developing a General Music Course

It should be assumed, from the beginning, that there is no one way to develop a General Music Course. A number of factors determine this: first, the background which the teacher brings to the class; second, the flexibility and versatility of the teacher; third, the backgrounds which the students bring to the class; fourth, the necessity to adapt the course as student needs are revealed; fifth, the facilities and equipment which are available; and sixth, the climate for a music program in the school.

Utilizing Teacher Skills

The special skills of the teacher will frequently determine the direction which this course will take. A teacher who graduated with an instrumental major will tend to develop the interest of the class in instruments and in instrumental music. A teacher who was a voice major in college will tend to interest the class in singing and vocal music. Any starting point is good if the teacher attempts to develop a pattern of musical growth, and students are exposed to a variety of musical interests and experiences.

Developing Student Interest and Skill

Some students achieve little in the field of performance. If, however, a student is given an opportunity to hold and produce a few tones on a trombone, a whole new world of sound is opened for him to explore if he so desires. Everyone can vicariously experience the thrill of creating and recreating music. The General Music Course is the place for such experiences. One need not be a Beethoven to appreciate the greatness of Beethoven.

The singing of an art song in unison can be a meaningful activity conducted under the direction of a skilled teacher. Through this experience students can learn to produce tones of beautiful quality, learn the difference between a strophic and a durchkomponiert song, contrast an art song with a folk song, and perhaps see and hear a film sung by one of the world's leading interpreters. The singing of rounds in a General Music Course can lead to real insights needed for an appreciation of counterpoint and the music of Johann Sebastian Bach. The more varied the experiences, the deeper the insights will go.

Listing the Functions of the General Music Course

There are three important functions for the General Music Course: one, to expose all of the students to the opportunities for making, creating and listening to music; two, to give students a general musical background to use as a basis for making musical choices; and three, to discover and encourage musical talent for continuing growth.

With regard to the first function, there should exist in the curriculum opportunities for the development of a course of study ripe with satisfying musical offerings. It matters little whether the course begins with singing and ends with a study of musical instruments, or whether the approach is logical or psychological. It is important, however, that the experiences open up for the students new insights inherent in learning. The second function, that of giving students a basis for making choices, is, in the highest sense, a revelation of musical growth. It may be that a talented singer has been motivated to take piano lessons in order to accompany himself or other singers, or in order to understand more completely the music which he is singing. Perhaps a clarinet student has come to see the need for help in music theory or creative writing, in order to make transcriptions, transpositions, or to better understand the music that he is playing. There is no limit to the background which a fine musician can develop. More than this, through the revelation of musical growth students can become aware of the continuous process through which they can enrich their lives. One of the joys of musical participation is the never—ending procession of exciting new activities related to performing and listening to music. All music lovers know the sheer joy of discovering a work by a master which is new to them. As they rehearse the music, the pleasure increases a thousandfold. Learning to make new choices, either as an amateur or a professional, can lead to additional experiences in music. The process is just as important as acquiring facts and information. Developing in students a positive attitude towards the making of choices is important.

With regard to the third important function of the General Music Course, that of discovering and encouraging musical talent, we know that the surface of the talent in our schools has scarcely been touched. Many gifted children are not discovered until the senior year of high school, and some are never discovered at all. All students can enrich their lives if the opportunities are there. When, early in the general education of the student, the teacher discovers a talent for singing, playing an instrument, conducting or writing music, the pupil can be directed to the specialty where fulfillment can be found.

Recruiting for the Specialties in the General Music Course

Recruiting for the specialties is a continuous process for the teacher. The General Music Course offers an ideal opportunity for finding, guiding, and developing gifted pupils. If the whole program grows out of and is connected with the General Music Course, the end result is that the entire curriculum is unified and supported by everyone, down to the last student. More talented students will rise to the top, and be better prepared, if there is a broad mass base to the program.

Utilizing a Wide Variety of Musical Experiences

The General Music Course, therefore, should create opportunities for all pupils to sing, handle and experiment with musical instruments, watch stimulating films and film strips, learn to use the signs and symbols of music, and listen to and learn about all sorts of music. With the new electronic devices available in the classroom, students can not only hear their own performances played back on tape recorders, but they can also hear the same music performed by the world's outstanding musical organizations on excellent electronic records and recording machines. The versatile music teacher takes advantage of this equipment and enhances the program in the General Music Course with it.

These well-chosen activities can build backgrounds for all of the students. The knowledge acquired will help students with the development of musical taste and serve as a basis for making intelligent choices. It has definitely been established that a growing interest in music is one of the best indications of an aptitude for music. We should exploit this knowledge to the hilt.

Contrasting the Logical and Psychological Approaches

The sequence of musical experiences in the course does not necessarily have to be logical. Sometimes a psychological approach, one which comes from a number of different directions, is more effective. A great deal depends upon the versatility of the teacher. One who can go off on a tangent, and then bring the group back again to the central idea, can create more excitement for music than one who is more rigid or formal. An instructor who knows how to shift skillfully from popular and folk music to a broader spectrum of offerings is an asset to the music staff.

Presenting Several Approaches to the General Music Course

The General Music Course can be organized for students in many ways. We cite here a few examples of approaches introducing music to beginners. In each case we indicate only a starting point. Each example has been developed into a full-length course of study, covering a semester or a year's work.

In one class the teacher announced that the topic for the semester was "Music in Daily Living." Together, the teacher and the students compiled a list of places in their daily living where people met music: radio, television, the theatre, movies, restaurants, weddings, funerals, churches, concert halls and dance halls. It was agreed that the list was incomplete, but other places could be added later. There were also special occasions and situations, it was agreed, in which music played a vital part. Some of these were listed: patriotic events, wars, peace meetings, love affairs, commemorative events, school graduations and many occasions where people gather together for a common cause. Out of these preliminary discussions came the beginnings of a course of study. Songs, recordings, films discussions, musical technics were implemented as needed. The large variety of musical experiences then began to create a need for new insights and skills. Students were motivated for further exploration and study. Topic after topic led to new avenues for musical and educational growth.

Another General Music Course centered its interest around the making of shepherd's pipes. The tools, tables, bamboo, and manuals for the building of pipes were provided. Through the enthusiastic leadership of the teacher, the class had to learn about the scale, decided upon the importance of ear training (shepherd's pipes must be tuned as they are made), and step by step learned to read music as the various holes in the instrument were added and fashioned. The class, in the process, learned about the physics of sound and learned to sing and play many folk songs. About Christmas time the group listened to the Trapp family playing traditional carols and singing Christmas music from all over the world. The group began to develop an interest in woodwind and other instruments of the orchestra. They planned a trip to the museum to see an exhibit of ancient instruments. In their diversity, these activities encouraged the development of musical insights and growth. The various lessons were rich in general information and related musical experiences, and the course paved the way for a series of choices which the students could make.

The popular music approach can also be good if it leads to the exposure of students to a wider range of musical experiences. It should lead to an understanding of many kinds of music and should meet the same requirements for musical growth found in other approaches.

A teacher of a General Music Course began with a popular song in another way. The class was asked to sing "The Man I Love" by George Gershwin. While learning the song, students discovered that Gershwin took the germ of a musical idea from the blues, developed it into a motive, then a theme, then a melody and finally into an art song. The attention of the class was focused on the skill with which the composer did this, and the technics which he used. They found that Franz Schubert did precisely the same thing when he wrote his famous "Ständchen" or

"Serenade." After dissecting the song by Schubert, the discussion of *what is a serenade* was postponed until Marian Anderson sang the song in German. A whole project grew out of taking the germ of a musical idea and developing it into a masterwork. The group heard another kind of Serenade, the *Eine Kleine Nachtmusik* of Mozart. The class also got to study the *Fifth Symphony* of Beethoven, the *Passacaglia in C Minor* by Bach, the *Fourth Symphony* of Tchaikovsky, the "Kyrie" from the *Mass in B Minor* by Bach and the Folk Opera *Down in the Valley* by Kurt Weill. In the process, the group sang a large variety of songs, listened to many recordings, watched appropriate films, compiled materials from newspapers and magazines for bulletin boards, did some reading in music history and literature, and examined how musical instruments were made. In a flexible program such as this one there was ample opportunity to introduce a wide range of materials, all pertinent and meaningful, and each one an avenue for musical growth.

For this teacher it was not enough for the class to sing popular and ethnic songs. Whatever was done in this General Music Course was meaningful musically and educationally, and served as a stepping stone for other musical experiences.

Relating the General Musical Course to a period in history being studied in the social studies class has also proven to be successful as an approach. Many songs, recordings, and films are available. The singing of such songs as "Battle Hymn of the Republic," "Goober Peas," "Tenting Tonight" can lead all the way to an Ives composition based on Civil War tunes. From the presentation of the bugle, which was used during the Civil War to play "Taps," it is easy to get into a discussion of the construction of brass instruments. From the study of fifes and drums a class can easily progress to other instruments of the band and orchestra. An entire course could evolve, one which would include nomenclature, note-reading, and even elementary theory.

Relating music to history has always proven of interest to students. In American history, as in world history, much music has grown out of the various crises. George Washington was familiar with the minuets of Josef Haydn's time and he certainly knew the early American reels. The songs of Francis Hopkinson were popular and the harpsichord and clavier were known in early America. As our nation pressed westward a new music of the frontier began to appear. There are many lively tunes from this era to be sung in the class. The social life of Dolly Madison in the White House included much music. The times of Abe Lincoln, the Civil War, the Reconstruction Period, the Spanish American War, two World Wars, all produced music which faithfully recorded the temper of the times. Here, again, entire units of work and whole courses of study can be developed, through which pupils can be motivated and can grow.

Using Popular, Folk, and Ethnic Music

It might be good at this point to discuss the place of popular, folk, and ethnic music in the curriculum. Since this music has at its command the various means of mass communications, it has now become "popular" in its truest sense. Popular music has truly become the folk music of the big city. Folk and ethnic music are gradually being integrated and blended into the mainstream of American life. The singing of old and new ballads, in its new popularity, has made it difficult to see where the folk and ethnic music ends and the popular music begins. It is more important to understand that this music is alive, vibrant, and potent with promise for use in the curriculum. It can be tied up with the past and with current history, and can be compared favorably with similar music from other eras and other parts of the world. Its inclusion in the curriculum is important. It should not be studied only for its own sake, but also because it is an asset for taking students, through the subject matter of the songs, into an unlimited number of related musical experiences. In the General Music Course the teacher should consistently talk about the relationship between music and people. This is what popular music is all about—music and people. A teacher can no longer refuse to use it in the classroom. It has now been commonly accepted as another kind of music through which we can establish new avenues for learning.

All subject matter that is pertinent to the essence of developing new insights in the study of music should be included. The study of jazz, rock and roll, soul music, and other popular forms has its place in the curriculum. We should guard, however, against permitting any small segment of the music field to take an undue amount of time out of the schedule. Unless there is careful planning, the teacher may end up with an exciting course in progressive jazz to the exclusion of other important material. We should not include progressive jazz, or anything else for that matter, in a music class merely to appease, entertain, or amuse students. Popular music, in itself, is important, but each part in the pattern should take its proper place by contributing to the development of a many-faceted curriculum.

Arranging a Balanced Content in the General Music Course

In planning the course of study for the General Music Course care should be taken to arrange a series of units which are coherent and balanced. These lessons do not necessarily have to follow in a logical sequence, but transitions from unit to unit should be made with ease.

Through thorough planning, students can be led to see and sense achievement as each unit is completed. Of utmost importance also is the thoroughness with which a subject is covered. Children can learn with a depth of appreciation and understanding, at whatever level they find themselves.

Encouraging Students to Explore in Music

The wealth of music material that is available is unlimited. Experienced teachers, at best, can serve as resource persons to direct students to the vast accumulation of the world's culture. We cannot hope to teach students all that there is to learn. We should encourage and develop habits of research, utilizing sources other than the teacher, and thereby helping students to the enjoyment of the heritage which is theirs to use.

How much singing should be included in the course? How much listening? How many films? The teacher is the most experienced and qualified person to evaluate all of the factors involved. Despite the need for careful planning, the teacher should seem to "play the course by ear." A great deal must depend upon the advancement of the group, its enthusiasm and interest. Here, again, the instructor should guarantee that the students are exposed to a large variety of musical experiences, those which invite individual participation and encourage active listening.

Utilizing the World Scene and Daily Living as
A Setting for a Course of Study

There are many approaches, then, to setting up a course of study for the General Music Course. Suggestions to the teacher for new avenues of learning can come from radio, television, the movies, newspapers, and magazines. All around us history is being made; a presidential inauguration or convention, the death of a Cardinal, the wedding of a princess, the coronation of a king, the assassination of a president or beloved leader. New developments in science, art, history, literature—any exciting thing which manifests itself in our daily living can be a starting place. Music is used all about us, as a part of these events, and is very much in evidence. Surely, the funeral of President John F. Kennedy, telecast from Washington, could have made a magnificently moving music lesson. The inclusion of some of the world's greatest music as a part of the service heightened the emotional significance of the ceremony, and made the impact of the occasion more meaningful. Here was an opportunity for the music teacher to point up dramatically the importance of music in our daily living as a comforter. Dramatizations of subject matter are as important in the music class as anywhere in the curriculum.

Using the Language of Music as a Means of Communication

Utilizing the language of music in the General Music Course has been greatly misunderstood. Certainly the signs and symbols of music should be presented so that students are familiar with them. A staff, a clef, notes, phrase marks, rests, and other symbols are the means by which a composer communicates ideas to an interpreter, and in turn to the listener. The newly initiated students in the General Music Course cannot learn to use all of these symbols immediately, but the understanding of their significance can help them to learn what the composer had in mind when composing the music. Just as a poet uses words, accents, rhythms, and rhyme, the musician uses his language to present musical ideas which he wants to convey. In this class, it is possible to use skeleton scores, so that the group can not only hear, but also see, how the music flows. Also in this class, the group can sing a melody of a Bach chorale-prelude, and at the same time hear the counterpoint played by a major symphony orchestra. As the orchestral music weaves in and out, and around what the pupils are singing, they are learning to follow a melodic line and are simultaneously developing insights into a magnificent piece of music written by a master craftsman.

Using Note-Reading as One Type of Musical Experience

An introduction to note-reading, however, is just one of the many musical experiences which newcomers have in the General Music Course. More specialized sight-reading belongs elsewhere in the curriculum, perhaps in the music theory class, choir, vocal ensemble, and instrumental classes. Teachers in the General Music Course, therefore, should concentrate on building an interest and enthusiasm for participating in a number of musical activities.

Teaching Students to Evaluate Their Musical Experiences

Part of the progress of growing up musically should include a period of evaluation by the teacher and the students. Pupils should be taught to take stock periodically of their musical growth. This is not so much a summarization as it is an evaluation of where they were, where they are now, and where they are going. Here, young people must come to see that their activities are a part of participating in a larger scheme of things. They must see that music is a part of eating, sleeping, socializing, studying, working, fantasying; that music makes their lives more meaningful; that the very air which they breathe has music in it—the sound waves! What a wonderful way to introduce the science of acoustics!

Meeting Musical Needs Through a General Music Course

Children come to school from varying socio-economic backgrounds, with musical talents of varying degrees. These talents fall into three categories: first, the large group of pupils who learn to use music in their daily lives without specializing; second, those talented amateurs who are quite proficient, but will use music as an avocation; and third, the gifted students who will tend to specialize and "professionalize."

Pupils in all three categories should have the General Music Course. The large majority of them need it because it may be their only direct contact with a balanced variety of musical experiences. The talented amateurs need the course because it will give them a basis and background for better musicianship and understanding. Those students who tend to specialize will need the General Music Course to broaden their horizons and give them a background for making the most intelligent and sophisticated interpretations.

Teachers have just begun to experiment with the place of General Music in the curriculum. There are still many questions to answer. We have gone far in our approach to the establishment of the specialties in music education. The time has now come to coordinate all of the courses in the music department and relate them to each other, so that the General Music Course becomes the basic program out of which the whole curriculum grows.

Three

Developing the

Vocal

Music Program

Capitalizing on the Universality of Singing

The singing of young children in the elementary school has universal appeal. The joy which they are expressing is often reflected in the excitement which shines in their faces. Music educators capitalize on this love for singing, which unfortunately, however, sometimes breaks down in the junior high school. It is common practice to blame the changing voice or the adolescent personality. Problems related to the use of the changing voice are not new. Many teaching devices and technics, appropriate for the junior high school age group, have been developed and are being used to advantage. A number of text books and much published singing material which deal with the problem are available. It is enough to say here that children of all ages love to sing and teachers have coped with the problem.

Channeling Potential Singers into a Vocal Program

Music teachers in the senior high school can always find a section of the student body which loves to sing. Many of these students are talented and need little motivation to join musical organizations. Our concern here is with the majority. What can be done to capture and maintain the interest of those who need re-motivation? As a large number of junior high school students move into the high school it is found that an interest in singing tends to lag. Those pupils who have discovered the General Music Course, and have a potential for learning to sing better, also need to be encouraged to join singing classes. Teachers can find in the high school large resources of raw material to be channeled into the vocal music program, where there are avenues for musical growth.

Knowing and Understanding the Adolescent Voice

Working with the adolescent requires special knowledge and skill. The changing voice is related to the changing, "bursting at the seams" personality. Surely, the physical growth of the larynx has a great deal to do with how one manipulates the voice in singing. Teachers on the high school level cannot afford to limit themselves to those children whose voices are completely changed. The high school music courses are committed to a program of assistance and development as students appear with an assortment of singing problems.

Planning for a Wide and Balanced Vocal Program

In some respects, the vocal music program is the easiest to develop. Music teachers know that almost everybody can sing. This gives the instructor an immediate starting point for teaching people to sing better. All kinds of vocal classes can be set up to meet these needs. In a large high school, where there may be a number of vocal music teachers, the program can capitalize on their skilled specialties. One teacher may have a fine background in the field of concert and opera; another may be an excellent accompanist and coach; a third may be a fine choir and choral director. Frequently, all of these skills can be found in one trained individual. Conditions in each school will vary, of course, but generally speaking, almost every high school can initiate a variety of vocal courses with ease and dispatch. The teachers, therefore, must together plan for a wide and well-balanced singing program.

Placing the Choir and Other Vocal Specialty Groups in Proper Perspective

The concert choir is perhaps the most popular activity in the voice department. It needs little expansion in size and quality. These advanced groups have come as far as we can expect. True, we can polish a little here and there, but basically the strides taken in the development of the high school choir have been phenomenal. When the founders of the Music Educators National Conference first organized to bring music to large masses of students they could not have conceived of such a high degree of specialization as exists in the high schools of the United States today. Publishers have prepared numerous volumes dealing with the organization, methods and materials, programming, and philosophy of the choir in music education. Colleges give specialized courses to train directors in the skills needed to maintain standards which reach greater heights each year. The choir has become the most advanced choral group in the school and in many cases in the community.

Teaching a Choir How to Acquire a Beautiful Tone

More efficient methods can improve the singing and musical development of school choruses. Choral directors should be well-prepared for the skilled tasks ahead of them. Special technics, for example, are needed to improve the sound of a singing group. Beginning with the initial rehearsal, a choir should be aware of beautiful tone and how to acquire it. One of the quick ways of achieving a sensitive sound is to balance the parts off, against each other, while working for effective blending. This is sometimes difficult because of an imbalance of numbers in any given part. There are devices to help blend the individual voice parts of the group. Conductors find that altos and tenors can often double for each other in part singing. In this way the conductor strengthens a weak melodic line or a part important to the harmony. Training a choir to sing softly, with good support, proves to be an asset at the rehearsal. It helps with the development of good tone and with the developing of a wider range of dynamics. Singers have difficulty in hearing how they actually sound, and it is here that the regular use of a tape recorder helps. Corrections can be made very quickly after playbacks, and choir members can learn to recognize good tone when they hear it.

Using Tone Blending

Tone blending, in addition, helps to develop uniform sounds, without which a balanced effect cannot be achieved. The choral conductor should work for a clear vowel sound on each note. All four parts should be produced with a round frontal quality which is identical. If the group is singing "He Watching over Israel" by Felix Mendelssohn, for example, students in all voice parts, whatever their individual notes may be, should produce them on H*ee*, W*ah*, Tch*eeng*, *Uh*-oo, V*uh*-r, *Ih*, z*rah*, E*h*-1, with the lower jaw dropped and with each vowel sensed high in the mask. Balancing and blending come from a combining of all parts into a uniform quality of sound. Clear, rounded vowels need not be exaggerated at performances, but they must be there.

Figure 3–1: *"He Watching over Israel," from* Elijah *by Felix Mendelssohn*

Figure 3–2: *The concert choir is one of the most popular activities in the Music Department*

Teaching Music Reading for Part Singing

One of the places where the rehearsal can break down is in the learning of voice parts. Much time can be wasted while the conductor drills the altos or the basses. For this reason, sectional practice periods are always more desirable. If facilities are not available for section leaders to work with their groups, it is better to call individual sectional meetings, in place of full rehearsals, in order to learn difficult sections of the music. Here, choir members should learn to read as well as sing the parts. Most disciplinary problems can be solved by keeping the various sections of the choir busy at rehearsals.

Part of each practice session should be spent on music reading. Learning to follow and read the score is important in the development of the choir's musicality. Here, much of the morale of the group is dependent upon knowing what is in the music, so that eventually parts are sung with accuracy and with strict adherence to what the composer put down on paper. It is to the advantage of the choir to be able to read a new piece of music at sight. While it is true that some drill is required in part singing, the greater the reading facility, the quicker the music begins to hang together.

Whether students learn to read with *sol-fa* syllables, numbers, note-names, a neutral syllable, or whether they use the movable or fixed *Do* system, is of little importance to the choir. Students, if they apply themselves, can learn to read in any system. In the United States we have been using the movable system for many years and it seems to get results. Of greater import, however, is the flow of the reading which is achieved. Any system which accomplishes this aim is worth using.

Making Music from the Beginning

From the beginning of reading at sight, the attempts should be musical. Attention to flow, accents, and phrasing helps the students along. Facility comes with practice. Frequently, reading a phrase with a neutral syllable will achieve the desired effects without too much drill. The approach to sight-reading should be informal and should utilize real music as much as possible. Solfeggio exercises on the high school level can become a real bore and should be avoided, if possible. Learning to read music, however, is valuable and the development of reading skills is important.

Planning the Seating and Standing Arrangements

The planning of the seating or standing chart should place the group in the classroom or on the stage for the best blending of sound. High school choral directors have been experimenting with various place arrangements, sometimes with the boys in front and the girls in back; at other times, boys in the middle front surrounded by girls on three sides. Several professional conductors, recently, in order to achieve a high degree of balance and to develop the independence of individual part singing, have been arranging the voice parts by standing them in quartets of soprano, alto, tenor and bass, and alternating each group in periodic sequence, as shown in Figure 3-3.

A more recent, uncommon arrangement used by many choral directors is illustrated in Figure 3-4.

Another arrangement used effectively by some groups is that presented in Figure 3-5.

A traditional one, indicated in Figure 3-6, can have a number of variations.

The seating arrangement which is chosen is not, in itself, important, but is only of value when it contributes to the balance and beauty of the choir tone. Choral instructors should experiment with seating positions in order to impress upon the choir the fact that tonal balance must be achieved. The standing or seating arrangement can help improve the musical end result.

Facing Rehearsal Problems

The musical training of choir singers often grows out of problems as they arise at the rehearsals. Many choral directors lift the rhythmic or dynamics difficulty out of the context of the composition and invent a short drill which will help the group to overcome the hurdle. Posthaste, the phrase is reinserted into the piece where it takes on new meaning. Rhythmic training is related to how the music flows, and students should be encouraged to look at the score to discover the correct way the music should sound. It is easier to do all of this at sectional rehearsals. In all practice periods, however, the choir should learn to sing the music as the composer intended it to sound. The finished product should be musical!

Placing the Emphasis on the Music

Many choirs spend some time on exercises in order to improve tone and musicianship. Usually the group achieves its goal in the exercises. The director must repeat the drilling for the same objectives in building the repertoire. Why not spend more time on the music itself? After a brief warm-up, perhaps utilizing an exercise or drill, it is more desirable to arrive at the beauty of the music by going directly to the melodic, har-

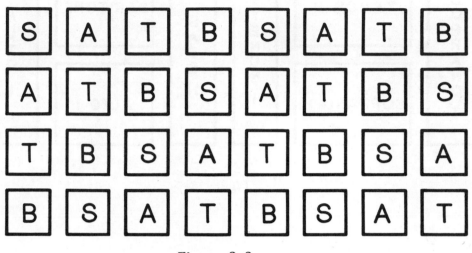

Figure 3–3

Figure 3–4

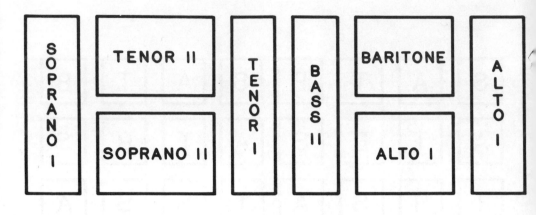

Figure 3–5

Figure 3–6

monic, and rhythmical content as designed by the composer. This serves two purposes: it prevents the rehearsal from becoming dull, and the music and its content are learned more quickly. *Always, the emphasis should be on the music.*

Conducting the Rehearsal

Each leader develops his own technics for conducting a rehearsal. Practice periods, as well as concerts, should be rewarding experiences. While drill is important, it is the musical way in which the group carries forward a particular phrase or musical sentence that makes it exciting. Often, when the choir has reached an impasse in a difficult section of the music, it may be best to set it aside for a while. The music will seem less difficult when it is approached again at the next rehearsal. When practice periods become unusually tense, especially after a long period of work, it is best to lighten the work with a short piece in which the mood is changed. Experienced teachers know the importance of periodically changing the activity in order to maintain interest.

Another clue to the achievement of higher morale is to practice the music without talking too much about it. To indicate to the choir how the tenor part flows here, or the alto part there, is more important than to talk about musicianship. Individual members of the choir are not always trained musically. Showing a singing group how to attain a musical effect, such as contrasting a legato with a staccato, can be quickly illustrated without making a speech about it. The less we talk and the more we sing, the better.

Developing Built-in Disciplines

There are disciplines, not of a musical nature, to be learned from participating in choral activities: how to sit, how to stand, how to walk in and out, how to hold the music, and how to conduct one's self generally. The necessity for watching the conductor and for knowing the music well is important. A concerted effort in this direction should culminate in a good performance. The singing of the group will only be as good as the combined individual efforts make it, so there cannot be too great an emphasis on self-discipline. The morale of the individual members and the group has a serious effect on how the music finally sounds.

Organizing the Practice Period

The morale of the choir will also depend upon how well organized the director is. If the preparation for a rehearsal is planned, the practice period is more likely to go smoothly. The distribution and collection of the music, the announcements, advance notice of special rehearsals and concert dates, all help choir members to make their personal schedules without conflicts. In an active music education program the choir director has many activities for which he is responsible. How well organized he is will determine how well he meets his obligations to all of them.

Developing Morale in a Singing Group

The organization of any choral group should have in it the seeds of a security which breeds high morale. The spirit of the group and the enthusiasm of the audience are raised by a repertoire of music which has contrasts and variety. Students need not wait for a concert to get a feeling of accomplishment, but should be able to sense achievement as rehearsals proceed. A heightened spirit in the choir comes directly from the sense of a job well done after a period of intensive work. If the choir activities are systematically organized to develop avenues for working together for the common good, the result will be improved music making.

Involving Choir Members in Organizational Problems

Members of singing groups should be involved in the solving of organizational problems. Each member of the choir can serve on some working committee to help with the routines for carrying on the operation of the group. A library committee distributes, collects, mends, and files music; a records committee assists with roll taking, record keeping, making contact with latecomers and absentees, and referring irregularities to the director; the robe committee distributes, collects, and keeps records on uniforms, robes, stoles, and jackets; a social committee plans parties, outings, and greeting cards for ill members. Some school musical organizations will require additional committees. The greater the involvement of the members the better. These responsibilities, along with the musical accomplishments of the group, will help to build morale.

Developing a Choral and Vocal Library

The choral director is constantly searching for new materials and making lists of his own for future use. A permanent library, varied in content, is essential. The music chosen should not be all of one school. It is desirable that compositions of contrasting style be listed, including concert, operatic, folk, modern, and popular pieces. The scores, however, should be superior musically, regardless of the difficulty, and should be within the technical and artistic grasp of the group. High school choirs, no matter how inexperienced or underprivileged, can always meet the standard if the music is rewarding and exciting. The great wealth of material which is available gives the director a variety of choices. Filed and indexed scores kept in the permanent library are available on a moment's notice for periodic repeat performances.

Building a Repertory of Choral Compositions

Developing a repertoire of great music is important in making students familiar with the standard literature. One large city high school, which at one time drew its student population from a high socio-economic grouping, now caters to students who come from underprivileged homes. It still maintains a good choir, one which each year includes in its repertoire standard classical and modern choral masterpieces. The group prides itself in the fact that for 53 years it has always closed its Christmas concert with the singing of the "Hallelujah Chorus" from *The Messiah* by George Frederick Handel. Each year additional choral and solo excerpts from this great oratorio are added as a part of the program. The permanent repertoire of the group includes works by such divergent composers as Mendelssohn, Brahms, Copland, Theron Kirk and Leonard Bernstein. High school students can inevitably reach out for and perform music which is of the greatest worth.

Initiating Unskilled Singers in Choral Groups

The choral director, if he is aware of the forces vibrating about him, accomplishes more in the long run when he periodically initiates unskilled students in the choral art. Novices can be taught to perform in a musical way. It is an important function of the director to introduce as many students as possible to the joys of singing. There is a great wealth of concert literature, both old and new. Singing it to the best of their ability can lead pupils to an appreciation of the music deeper than that of just listening. Senior students graduate each year. Their places should be filled, if possible, with ninth- and tenth-grade students to allow for a longer period of growth in the choir.

Relating the Choir Program to the Curriculum in General Education

The highly skilled choir does, of course, have its place in the complete music curriculum. In its specialization, however, it must never be aloof, above, or detached from the remainder of the program. It must never get so big or exclusive that it becomes an appendage of the school program. There are some schools in which the choirs perform in churches, community centers, for service organizations, men's and women's clubs, and rarely perform for their fellow students. The choir should become a school educational activity first, and an outside service organization second. No activity functioning for the general education of the students should take on the form of an up-ended pyramid. When the choir loses its educational function it no longer belongs in a school.

In a large, academic high school, in the western part of Pennsylvania, the entire music program centered around three excellent choirs, three excellent orchestras, and three excellent bands. The training of these groups was on a high level. The tenth-grade choir was a feeder group for the eleventh-grade choir. Both groups served to prepare candidates for the highly specialized senior group. In examining the entire music schedule, however, it was found that there were no general music classes, theory and harmony classes, music appreciation, music literature or music history courses. The entire music curriculum involved approximately 550 pupils in a school population of 3,600 pupils. The teachers involved in this program performed very well in a limited curriculum. The excellent musicianship displayed by the three choirs was beyond criticism; the schedule superb, as far as it went. But what about the other 3,000 students who could be motivated to enjoy some kind of music? At best, this program catered only to some of the most gifted students. Pupils with other talents could find little opportunity for training within the school. A motivated solo singer, for example, had to seek training after school hours outside of the school at a conservatory. Many students are unable to pay for lessons and an opportunity should be provided for developing their talents. Often, it has been found, when talent is discovered in the General Music Course, it is better nurtured in the school, before being referred to a conservatory for more specialized training. If additional vocal teachers are not available to conduct related singing activities, an over-sized choral program should be consolidated to allow teacher time for the expansion of the curriculum. Students in the school should have an opportunity to choose from a variety of offerings through which they can develop their talents.

Directors of choral groups in the high schools are to be commended for the great progress made in the last 50 years. This is an area in music education which reaches a large number of pupils, and it must be included in the music curriculum. The director must come to view it as an integral part of the whole program.

Preparing a Vocal Program Which Meets the Needs of All of the Students

Not every student will qualify for the concert choir. In some of the larger schools we also find junior choirs, vocal ensembles, boys and girls glee clubs, and combined glee clubs. Motet and madrigale groups can also be found functioning here and there. All of these activities become highly specialized and are organized on the same basis as the choir. Teachers of these groups concern themselves with organization, methods and materials, programming, standards, morale, and disciplines. It is to these groups that the majority of the pupils gravitate. There is an opportunity here in the broadened schedule to search out talent, to direct pupils to a variety of courses, and to refine tastes. A number of these students eventually will find their way into the choir where they can serve with experience and distinction.

Organizing Voice Classes

Few high schools have been able to set up classes in voice instruction. The absence of this specialty in the schedule is unexplainable, unless, perhaps, it is due to a lack of teachers' time. For a number of years most high schools have had classes in instrumental instruction, where individual instruments are taught and credit is given. Why not voice? The growth of the instrumental program, of course, stems from the importance attached to the marching band. Vocal teachers must now stress the importance of the voice class. With a large variety of interests in singing, from grand opera to the finest in popular music, we should have little trouble in setting up the voice class which gives credit for each semester of work.

There is a wide interest in voice training. Radio, television, the record player, and modern stereo recordings have built an enthusiasm for singing. The voice class can meet this need. Modern electronics and technology have built an interest in concert, opera, religious, folk, and popular songs. Teachers have a responsibility for setting standards in all fields of singing. They should aim to improve skills. Many students, in the name of style, tend to ignore reasonable standards of voice production. The wear and tear on their voices is unfortunate. Teachers should aim to improve musicianship in the field of popular singing as well as in concert music. There is a need for getting new singers started with good vocal habits. In this course, individual attention is given to the students who have moved towards a kind of personal music making.

The organization of the voice class should be kept simple. Classes of eight students are ideal. Here the teacher develops technics for teaching proper breathing, opening the mouth, producing and sustaining the tone on clear vowels. How to support the tone in phrasing must be practiced. Developing better musicianship for correct pitch, securer tone, more effective song singing is encouraged. Building a repertoire of concert, religious, patriotic, and modern songs is an essential part of the course.

Building a Repertory for Voice Students

An opportunity should be provided in the vocal music program to study music written for the theatre. This activity includes learning selections from opera, musical comedy, light opera, and a variety of other music for the stage. These musical selections and scenes capture the imagination of adolescents. Setting up opportunities for learning and participation insures a new avenue for musical growth.

Experience has proven that high school students can present excerpts from opera and even carefully selected complete operas. A number of high schools have given fine performances of *Down in the Valley* by Kurt Weill, unaltered and unabridged. Scenes from *Don Giovanni* by Mozart, utilizing the duet, "La Ci Darem la Mano" and the arias, Don Giovanni's "Serenade" and Zerlina's "Batti, Batti, O, Bel Masetto," have been performed successfully in high school. Various scenes from *Carmen* by Bizet have been presented by high school students. Included were "Habanera" for mezzo-soprano and chorus, "Toreador Song" for baritone and chorus, and the "Card Scene" for mezzo-soprano and quintette. The entire "Kermesse" scene from *Faust* by Gounod, utilizing chorus, ballet, and soloists, has been effectively staged. Duets from *Lakme, Traviata,* and *Norma* are within the ability of some high school students. "Solenne in Quest' Ora" from *La Forza del Destino* by Verdi is a powerful duet within the range of high school boys. Excerpts from lighter works such as *The Bartered Bride* by Bedrich Smetana, *La Percole* by Offenbach, *Martha* by von Flotow, and *Die Fledermaus* by Johann Strauss, all have been performed on high school stages.

Supervising Voice Training and Practice

High school students should not strain on this vocal material. Only where there is a voice teacher equipped to supervise this training should the activity be included in the program. These selections are listed here to indicate that students of high school age have performed them well. In many schools it is not possible to have an opera workshop. Students can be trained in voice classes to sing arias, duets, trios, and other selections from opera. With the assistance of the school orchestra and ballet groups, fine operatic programs can be planned. Full-length operas are difficult to produce, but there is no reason why excerpts cannot be staged. Actually, operatic music is more effective on the stage for which it was written. In Philadelphia, the City Wide Opera Workshop has presented scenes from *The Magic Flute* by Mozart and a new opera, *William Penn,* by Romeo Cascarino.

Overtaxing the Voice

There are those who believe that we should not tax the voices of high school students in the singing of such heavy works. Not too long ago it was the policy of voice teachers not to permit the training of the changing boy's voice at all. The argument usually came from those teachers who were not equipped to handle the problems of the adolescent singer. Certainly, a teacher who knows his business would never permit a student to misuse his voice. Today, voice teachers believe that boys and girls can be trained throughout the changing voice period.

Scheduling Advanced Vocal Training for Gifted Students

We have a precedent for this type of instruction. Luisa Tettrazini made her operatic debut at the age of 16; Lilli Lehmann at 18. Angelica Catalani, Maria Malibran, and Adelina Patti sang their first operatic performances at 17. Carl Maria von Weber chose Henriette Sonntag to sing the title role of *Euryanthe* at the age of 17. The voices of young boys were treated no differently in those days. Enrico Caruso began to sing publicly at the age of ten. He continued his lessons, singing throughout the changing voice period, professionalizing until he reached maturity. Manuel Garcia, the famous Spanish tenor and teacher, made his professional debut at the age of 17. Certainly, with new electronic devices at our command, we should be able to train students to learn excerpts and complete roles without strain and hardship. All of these recommendations are made with one reservation: the adolescent voice must be in the hands of a teacher who knows how to handle the delicate problem safely.

Using Music Written for the Theatre

There is much vocal music written for the theatre, very beautiful scores by Richard Rodgers, Jerome Kern, Irving Berlin, Leonard Bernstein, and others too numerous to name. Students enjoy singing these songs. In the history of our folk and popular music, young people have always turned to these selections as an opportunity for self-expression. The music teacher should help high school students to sing them more effectively.

Developing Small Vocal Ensembles

From time to time there will arise the need for developing smaller ensembles such as trios, quartettes, quintettes, and a variety of other combinations. In developing scenes from musical shows, those which require smaller groups of singers, there are opportunities for working on a more intimate basis with students. Scenes such as "Standin' on the Corner" from *A Most Happy Feller* and "There Is Nothing Like a Dame" from *South Pacific* are good vehicles for a small group of boys. "Three Little Maids from School Are We" from *The Mikado* and "I'm So Pretty" from *West Side Story* are interesting scenes for a small group of girls.

The teacher of concert and operatic music and the teacher of popular singing all aim for good voice production. Styles of interpretation may vary, but the manipulation of the voice should be the same. The kinds of material sung will determine the style, but the voice production will depend upon the proper use of the vocal apparatus. Many opera singers, Dorothy Kirsten, Eileen Farrell, Helen Traubel, Jan Peerce, Robert Merrill, and others have from time to time performed popular music successfully. A number of popular singers, such as Kate Smith, Edie Adams, and Andy Williams have also performed concert music successfully. Most of the better popular singers study voice production with specialists in the field in order to save wear and tear on the voice. The well-equipped voice teacher should be able to help set standards in all phases of voice production.

Using Folk and Popular Music

Opportunities for expanding all kinds of activities in the vocal music area are unlimited. With recent developments in the folk music field, the sale of guitars has sky-rocketed, indicating that many more people are singing to the accompaniment of the guitar. What are the implications for the high school vocal music teacher? Obviously, he should become involved.

In one high school, a folk music club was formed for those students who played guitars and sang. This lead to the development of a folk singing group which improvised in harmony as they sang. The instrumental group included guitar, balalaika, banjo, harmonica players, and folk drummers. After a period of rehearsing, the group began to improve in its skills. Invitations to give concerts were received. Assisted by a student narrator, the group performed in school assemblies, public libraries, community churches, and synagogues. With the help of the teacher, recordings, and tape recorders, the standards of the group were gradually raised. More effective pitch accuracy, more subtle harmonies, clearer diction, and vocal articulation began to appear. A number of students were encouraged to study with experts in the field. Others grew in their interest and appreciation of many kinds of music. All students came to see this activity as another kind of music in which man can find an opportunity for self-expression and growth.

Involving a Large Number of Students in a Singing Activity

The teacher of singing has an opportunity to reach large numbers of students. The desire of young people to communicate with the world around them should be obvious to all who work in music education. Teachers in our public schools have to be more versatile and more flexible. If they look back at their own music education, and try to discover how they first developed an interest in music, they will be able to see more clearly how to guide young people today.

Building Morale, Character, and a Cultural Life

Short- and long-range goals, associated with a program of general education, have not been discussed here. Authorities in the field of general education can do this very well. It is important to state, however, that participating in a singing activity can help build morale, character, and a cultural life of worth. Whether this is done through the playing of an instrument, learning how to sing, or acquiring listening skills, there are many by-products of becoming involved in musical activities. The music teacher must be aware of them because this involvement will not always happen of its own accord. The teacher must nourish it.

The disciplines which come from participation should be positive. One of the finest musical programs ever assembled by amateurs was at a penitentiary in the east. It could boast of an excellent symphonic band, a good chorus, soloists, and a dance band. Nearly all of the participants had developed their musical skills before committing their felonies. Before music teachers can take credit for character building, they must be assured that an active, positive approach to music instruction is used, setting up disciplines which carry over into the daily lives of the students.

The music teacher has a ready-made opportunity to build a good vocal program. With his knowledge and skill he comes to a large market of raw materials, available and eager for development in enrichment courses. His versatility and interest in young people will help him to evolve a series of activities which will meet their needs.

Four

Developing the Instrumental Music Program

Positive Aspects of the Instrumental Program

The art of playing a wind instrument or beating out rhythms on a drum has become big business. Deserved credit for the phenomenon goes to the whole field of public school music. Some recognition must also be given to the manufacturers of musical instruments who annually make great efforts to advertise the component parts of the high school bands and orchestras. The sight and sound of the dance and stage band have also contributed to the sale of musical instruments and to the upsurge in enthusiasm for instrumental education.

Much good has come from this movement, which has made a permanent impression on the entire field of music education. The direct attraction for a trumpet or clarinet sets up motivations for students to practice endlessly during school hours, after school and at home. From the desire to play in a marching or dance band, there have evolved valuable by-products of a disciplinary nature which contribute to the ultimate success of the instrumental program. Students are given an opportunity to take part in an enriched cultural life, to develop friendships, to become involved in an active school and community spirit, and to grow musically as part of a common effort for the common good.

Lag Between Philosophy and Practice

There are some aspects of the development, however, which have been open to question. Recent studies reveal a lag between the development of a philosophy in music education and current practices. While the teachers believe in high standards of performance and an ever improving quality of instruction, the pressures of using instrumental organizations as public relations units sometimes defeat the objectives of the modern program. The philosophy advocates involving as many students as possible in the playing of musical instruments. However, the concerts, parades, and elaborate stage productions have, in the past, involved only a few specialized students and the best playing groups are usually chosen to perform.

There are indications that the gap between philosophy and practice is closing. Instrumental activities are taking their proper place in the general curriculum. School administrators are making serious attempts to eliminate abuses. The prime objective now seems to be moving away from the overemphasis on public relations and entertainment, and toward an educational approach which guarantees greater musical growth for more pupils.

When to Begin Instrumental Instruction

A program of instrumental instruction can best begin in the elementary school, continue through the junior high school and be supplemented on the senior high school level. The teaching of instruments should be available for all students who qualify at any level. It would be a mistake to discontinue instruction anywhere along the line. The organization of class instrumental instruction has evolved over a number of years, and teachers now seem to have arrived at common agreements as to when and where to begin. It is the practice to begin the instruction of stringed instruments in the third grade and brass and woodwinds lessons in the fourth. Percussion training, which begins earlier with the rhythm band, can be taught in all of the grades. Sometimes string specialists are employed on a part-time basis and travel from school to school giving instruction. At the high school level full time instructors can continue the training of those who have already begun to study in the elementary school and can also initiate newly motivated pupils.

Class Instruction

Instrumental classes vary in size and level of advancement. Classes of six to eight students function well and allow each pupil to move ahead at his own rate of speed. Although some highly skilled teachers have developed methods for instructing classes of larger size, it is reasonable to assume that the smaller the classes, the greater the opportunities for individual attention.

Necessity for Proper Facilities

Proper facilities for carrying on instrumental instruction can be of great help. Where practice rooms are available, the teacher can go from room to room instructing in one group, correcting the practice habits of another, and commending still another where the pupils are doing well. Some of these classes develop into small ensembles. The advantage of having such facilities is that it permits the grouping and regrouping of pupils so that a maximum of growth is allowed for each individual. With motivation, progress can be remarkable in a short period of time.

Importance of Ensemble Playing

Those school systems which nurture an early instrumental program develop well—skilled musical organizations in the high school. A broad program for the teaching of instruments guarantees a large number of applicants for the orchestra and band, students who may be directed to the various playing groups by the teacher. It is beneficial for instrumentalists to get the experience of playing in an ensemble. Some pupils get a great amount of pleasure from playing in smaller groups. Student needs differ, making it equally desirable for the violinist to play in a string quartet, or a trombone player to play in a dance band. A number of instrumentalists may desire to play in the marching band; others in a dance

Photo Courtesy CONN CORP., Elkhart, Indiana

Figure 4–1: It is beneficial for instrumentalists to get the experience of playing in an ensemble.

combo. Most students will want to perform in ensemble groups and music educators are aware of the tremendous opportunities for musical growth which exist with the organization of these activities.

Motivations for Playing an Instrument

The prospect of playing an instrument in an orchestra, marching band, or dance combo, therefore, is a positive motivating force in learning to play a musical instrument. Many pupils, recruited to take lessons in the elementary school, are encouraged by the hope of joining a performance unit. The dropout rate at the junior high school level, unfortunately, is high. Pressure to succeed, competition from more competent students, and ineffective methods of teaching are some of the causes for a loss of interest. Before beginning to study an instrument seriously, it is important for students to have contacts with a wide variety of instruments, to feel them, learn to manipulate them, and to learn how to produce a few musical tones. The wider the contacts with many instruments, the greater the motivations can become.

Technics, Materials, and Courses of Study

There are many music-series books, written for programmed instrumental instruction, for all instruments and for students on all levels. These courses of study have been tried and tested and are available for classroom use. Some are better than others and each meets a different need. There are, also, a number of traditional methods which are useful for continuing the advancement of pupils. One of the signs of growth is the movement from imperfection to greater facility. These graded materials help the student to become increasingly more proficient in his technics.

Scheduling Instrumental Classes

Despite difficulties in scheduling, instrumental classes have grown and expanded within recent years. Conflicts with academic subjects have pushed many of these groups to the outer fringes of the roster. In some ways this is a good thing because it allows for greater flexibility. Many more classes, before school, after school, and during school hours in the place of study periods, have resulted. In larger cities, area and district centers have been established to which pupils can be referred for instruction. City-wide, Saturday morning centers, sponsored by local school boards, have also begun to appear and the trend toward large summer instrumental programs has increased. This phenomenal growth speaks well for music education.

Courses of Study

It is difficult for instrumental instructors to write courses of study. The materials which a teacher uses are usually established, formal methods which have been published and accepted by leaders in the field. The instrumentalist is working in a performance area where success is measured mostly by how well the group sounds. The development of technics and skills takes a great deal of time and the instructor, in using graded materials, already has outlined courses which have been tried and tested. The teacher, in addition, builds a library of materials which are available for current and future use. New trends now indicate a need for curriculum guides for the instrumental program. It may not be too far in the future when most teachers will begin to list courses of study for instrumental groups.

The Development of the Marching Band

The flashy, colorful, carnival-like impression that a marching band makes is most attractive. The development of this group can be a most rewarding activity. Experience has shown that small bands can be placed on the football field in a short period of time. In one school, a 40-piece band performed at a football game after eight months of study. Most of the students were new at playing their instruments and inexperienced at playing in an ensemble. The band did not produce a half-time show, nor did it march to music. The group, however, was prepared to play a number of easy marches and fanfares and accompanied a number of school cheers. During the half-time period the group did march to the center of the field, accompanied only by the drums, and led the students in the stands in the singing of the Alma Mater. While it was true that the musical results were limited, the motivations were powerful. The music teacher knew how to use these with discretion. New applicants for the band and instrumental instruction seemed to come from all directions, and this performance marked the beginning of a fine band program which, as the years moved on, grew in size and stature.

Organized primarily for sports events, community parades and patriotic occasions, the marching band becomes the most glamorous activity in the music curriculum. Its potential for musical growth is unlimited. The great amount of time spent on half-time shows, parades, and the changing of uniforms, however, detracts from time available for greater

Figure 4–2: *The flashy, colorful impression that a march-band creates can help make the activity most rewarding*

musical development. The demand for appearances in the community limits the time of students for academic work. Playing in the outdoors, or in large armories, leads to the production of blasting sounds and loud drumbeating, to the detriment of purer tone and subtler interpretations. If, in addition, the band is periodically prepared to participate in contests, the many hours of rehearsals, both for playing and marching, become self-defeating. If we guard against some of these abuses, the band need not be the unmusical activity that it sometimes becomes. The effective band director tries to satisfy community needs while balancing the musical activity against the students' other necessary academic courses.

The Band and Community Relations

One must not underestimate the value of community relations or entertainment, however. It may be necessary to have a period of indoctrination in order to build community support. Many times, even though musical results are limited, this phase of the band's development may only be a passing one which eventually leads to the organization of the combined marching and concert band. Furthermore, a marching band which capitalizes upon its attractiveness can also place greater emphasis on musicality. It doesn't necessarily follow that a band that is well uniformed, drilled, or marched must play poorly. The group, through its director, can set its own standards. It can lead instead of follow in the development of public taste.

Figure 4–3: Band in $14,000 band shell built by Warren, Ohio football boosters

Photo Courtesy CONN CORP., *Elkhart, Indiana*

The Marching Band and the Concert Band

One of the ways in which a marching band can grow musically is by converting itself into a concert band which also marches. In this way its narrow repertoire is broadened to include works which require a more subtle type of musicianship and more advanced technics. Adding the symphonic literature to its repertoire impoves its whole image and compensates for the limiting aspects of other activities in its program. The contribution of the band, however, must be functional and educational. The musical growth of its members will be determined by how dedicated the director is to these cultural and educational objectives.

Selecting Literature for the Concert Band

A vast literature has become available for the symphonic band. Much of the orchestral catalogue has been transcribed and is available for groups at all stages of development. Each year new materials are being prepared and are added to the publications on hand. The importance of selecting appropriate music for the group cannot be overestimated. Attention must be given to the large variety of talents in the organization, and to the varied levels and backgrounds of the pupils. Choices should not be too difficult. Much of the materials has been organized and graded by reputable arrangers and publishers.

Conducting the Band Rehearsal

Each band director will develop his own technics for conducting a rehearsal. There are, however, a number of essentials, some of a nonmusical nature, which must be considered an important part of the practicing period and which help to pave the way for the musical development of the group. It is enough to say here that all of the minute details must be worked out in order for the rehearsal to go smoothly.

The conductor of a band or orchestra has a unique problem. In the instrumental ensemble the talent of the individual player helps to determine the success of the group. It is true that the skills must be coordinated and blended, but the technics which are built into each instrument and the knowledge which the leader must have of the individual technics involved will determine how well the group performs. It is difficult to build a good instrumental ensemble if the players have had poor training for the playing of instruments. An orchestra or band conductor, therefore, must be familiar with technics for the playing of all instruments and should be able to identify the source of a technical problem as it appears.

There are a few basic suggestions which will help to insure the smoothness of the rehearsal. The setting for practicing together is extremely important. The room should be large and allow for the resounding of the music without any distortion. It should be well lighted and well heated and provision should be made for proper ventilation. In order for the rehearsal to begin promptly, the student committee should set up the chairs and stands, and put out the music folders before the ensemble arrives. All of the mechanics for setting up the practice period should be taken care of in advance so that an efficient rehearsal can get off to a good start.

The format of the rehearsal need not be rigid, but there should be set procedures and patterns used which assist the disciplines necessary for an orderly rehearsal. Tuning the band, through the use of scale passages or any other device, must be an accepted pattern through which the students learn to listen and hear. In an instrumental ensemble the emphasis should be on group participation. As much as possible, every activity, including tuning, should be pursued together.

Directions by the teacher should be brief and concise so that most of the time is spent in rehearsing and playing. The conductor must periodically stop the orchestra or band to explain what the composer had in mind when he made specific notations. Students must learn to observe carefully the markings which a composer recorded. Players in an ensemble, as well as orchestra and band members, should learn to follow the hand signals of the conductor with regard to tempi, dynamics, and balance.

Seating Charts for Bands of Various Sizes

After the band leader has made a study of the musical resources available for the organization of the band, he must be concerned with seating arrangements which are functional and will produce the best blend of sound. None of the traditional seating charts are sacred. Often, in order to achieve a better balance of sound, the trumpets or the oboes may be shifted with more telling effects. Band leaders, however, have evolved what are now traditional seating arrangements. We list them in Figures 4-4 through 4-7 by size and instrumental combination.

Encouraging the Musical Growth of the Band

The band conductor has an opportunity to develop musicianship through tuning, the balancing of the tone and the dynamics, encouraging the technical development of the individual players, and developing an understanding of the music which the group plays. Sectional rehearsals, taking the band apart and putting it together again, can make for greater

SMALL BAND—20 TO 30 PLAYERS

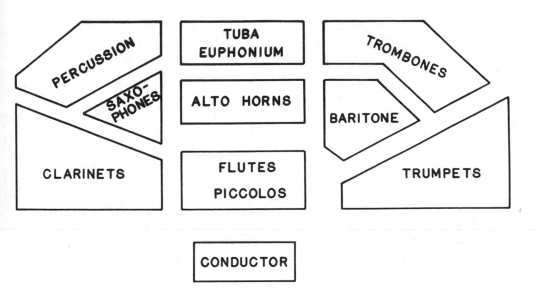

Figure 4–4

clarity and perfection. Devices which lead students to see how the music is created or evolves are important. Through the use of these technics the end product can become more musical. Everything that we do in music education should lead to this, a more meaningful musical experience.

If the director wants to encourage musical growth he can achieve the objective in the symphonic and marching band as well as in any other activity in the music curriculum. Everything that is accomplished, from the organization of the group to the final performance of the music chosen, is colored by the efforts of the leader to establish a growth process. His philosophy and objectives for the band can carry over into the entire music program and even influence the instrumental program in the elementary and junior high schools. The integration of this activity with a program in general education will result in the musical growth of all children, those who are performing and those who are listening. The concert and marching band, therefore, can become another avenue for the advancement of musical growth in the larger curriculum.

CONCERT BAND—30 TO 60 PLAYERS

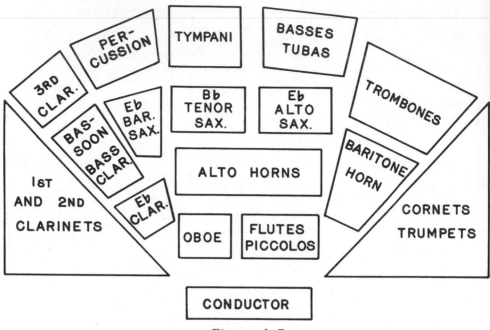

Figure 4–5

Organizing the School Orchestra

Organizing the school orchestra presents problems not unlike those of the band but with several added problems. The greatest challenge comes, of course, from the lack of competency of the strings at the high school level. Radio, television and the dance band have tended to glamorize the brass, woodwind and percussion instruments, and have encouraged a flight away from the strings. Secondly, one can achieve greater proficiency on band instruments in a shorter period of time. Thirdly, the standard repertoire of the orchestra tends to require a greater degree of skill for immediate results. Good performance demands a great amount of drill in order to develop a balanced sound. The tuning of the individual stringed instruments and the string section of the orchestra is also difficult. All of these factors tend to discourage students and listeners in the early stages of training. It becomes mandatory, therefore, that instrumental teachers build a program for recruitment and study in order to overcome the problem.

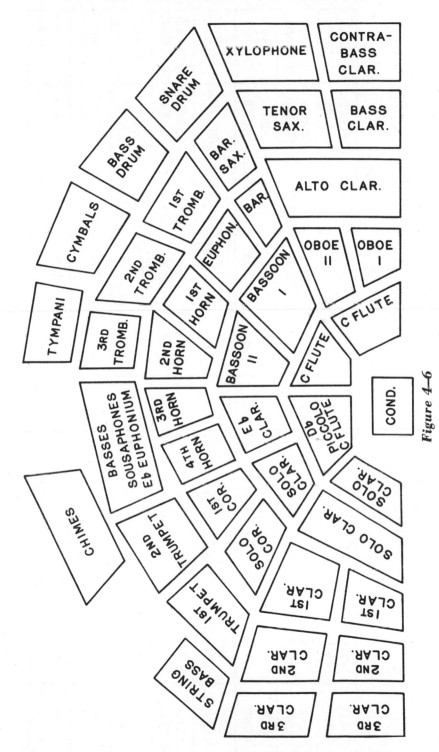

CONCERT BAND—70 to 100 PLAYERS

Figure 4–6

MARCHING BAND—80 PLAYERS

FIELD DRUM	1ST TROMB.	2ND TROMB.	BARITONE	BASSOON TEN. SAX.	ALTO CLAR.	2ND CLAR.	2ND CLAR.
FIELD DRUM	1ST TROMB.	2ND TROMB.	BARITONE	BASSOON TEN. SAX.	ALTO CLAR.	2ND CLAR.	2ND CLAR.
FIELD DRUM	1ST TROMB.	2ND TROMB.	BARITONE	TEN. SAX.	ALTO CLAR.	2ND CLAR.	2ND CLAR.
CYMBALS	BBb TUBA	3RD TROMB.	Eb TUBA	BAR. SAX.	BASSOON BASS CLAR.	3RD CLAR.	3RD CLAR.
BASS DRUM	BBb TUBA	BBb TUBA	Eb TUBA	BASS SAX.	BASS CLAR.	3RD CLAR.	3RD CLAR.
BASS DRUM	SOLO TROMB.	1ST TROMB.	2ND TROMB.	Bb SOP. SAX.	PICCOLO	SOLO CLAR.	SOLO CLAR.
GLOCKEN-SPIEL	SOLO TROMB.	1ST TROMB.	2ND TROMB.	Eb CLAR.	PICCOLO	SOLO CLAR.	SOLO CLAR.
FIELD DRUM	1ST HORN	2ND HORN	3RD TROMB.	1ST ALTO SAX.	1ST OBOE	1ST CLAR.	1ST CLAR.
FIELD DRUM	3RD HORN	4TH HORN	3RD TROMB.	2ND ALTO SAX.	2ND OBOE	1ST CLAR.	1ST CLAR.
FIELD DRUM	3RD HORN	4TH HORN	3RD TROMB.	2ND ALTO SAX.	2ND OBOE	1ST CLAR.	1ST CLAR.

DRUM MAJOR

Figure 4-7

Recruiting for the School Orchestra

Recruiting students for the instrumental classes, those who will eventually come into the school orchestra or band, is best done in the General Music Course. Demonstrations on the violin or cello can lead to an interest in the strings. Showing how the instrument is constructed and permitting individual pupils to produce tones on it makes for excitement. As the instructor takes apart a French horn, to show how it is built and how it operates, students develop an interest in all of the brass instruments. The making of shepherd's pipes or the playing of a recorder can lead to an interest in the woodwind family. Students whose voices are changing and who cannot be motivated to sing, often can be interested in learning to play an instrument. From this general music activity, therefore, a group of potentially talented and interested pupils can be recruited for specialization.

There are a number of additional ways to recruit for the school instrumental program. It is most helpful if the senior high school teacher has good communications with the elementary and junior high school instructors. He must periodically look for new candidates from these schools which feed into his program. Students who study with private instructors outside of the school can also be motivated to participate. Announcements can be made in the assembly, in all of the music classes, and particularly in those where instrumental instruction is given. These are the best sources of instrumental material.

Building an Interest in Playing Stringed Instruments

It has already been proven that an active interest in the strings can be developed. School orchestras are on the increase and the number of string players is slowly growing. In Japan, Professor Shinichi Sazuki, through a creative approach with young children, has developed a progressive school of violin playing which is influencing the development of string players all over the world. In this country, teachers in conservatories have been working along similar lines, developing an improved string program. This movement should eventually result in an increase in the number of string players at the high school level.

A large number of elementary school pupils are studying the violin in the big urban centers. The drop-out rate at the junior high school level is higher than it should be. Can this be the result of our teaching methods or materials? A child who is playing well and loves his instrument does not tend to give it up. Since it is difficult to get musical results from an instrument in which the technics get in the way, methods must be devised so that technics can be taught with rapidity and ease. A program must be organized to eliminate the frustrations associated with overcoming the technical problems involved, so that the child can learn to make music on his stringed instrument as quickly as possible. Instrumental teachers in the elementary and junior high school are re-thinking and re-organizing the string program for more effective results.

Making a Start with the High School Orchestra

Once the problems connected with the strings have been tackled, we can go on to look at other difficulties related to the organization of the orchestra. The high school orchestra, in the beginning, will not always have the proper variety of instruments for a balanced sound. Music educators are already familiar with procedures in which an alto saxophone can substitute for a French horn, or a baritone saxophone can take the place of a bassoon. In some schools substitute instruments make the difference between having an orchestra or not. Most instrumental instructors realize that there are decided advantages to using replacements in order to give students a worthwhile musical experience. Clever arrangers and transcribers have been busy in music education and perform a creditable job in making it possible for a balanced school orchestra to function. It is more desirable, of course, to develop a complete complement of instruments for the school symphony orchestra. Until a balanced group is achieved, however, the teacher uses available instruments to attain the best possible sound.

The Wide and Varied Background of the Conductor

The orchestra and band conductor must have a broad background of instrumental technics and an understanding of educational psychology in order to cope with these difficulties. The wider and more varied the background of the teacher, the more it is likely that the tone will improve. The quicker and more directly the leader gets to the root of the problem, the better. Several years ago, Leopold Stokowski was invited to a rehearsal of a very good city-wide high school orchestra. The group was rehearsing his transcription of the "Passacaglia in C Minor" by Johann Sebastian Bach. Within half an hour Mr. Stokowski showed the violin section how to get a more luscious vibrato, the clarinet section was briefed on how to articulate their parts more clearly, and the whole group was taught to play with greater precision. He knew exactly how to tell the orchestra in a few words what was needed to improve the balance and the tone. His broad background and experience with achieving tonal colors helped him to communicate to the group the technics for producing a better sound. The end result was truly amazing.

The Development of a Singing Tone in the Orchestra

The development of a singing tone in the orchestra should be paramount. The instrumental conductor must know how to achieve a singing, balanced, and blended tonal cluster. The leader, in addition to having a knowledge of how to play each instrument, must also be able to recognize aurally what the acceptable quality of each instrument is and be able to show the student how to achieve it. If the leader is at all times conscious of tone quality the members of his group will catch the fever.

There are a number of elements which contribute to the development of a singing tone. First, as in singing, correct breathing is important in the playing of woodwind and brass instruments. Articulation, phrasing, and the sustaining of the tone depend greatly upon learning to breathe deeply while maintaining correct posture for supporting the tone. The importance of a correct embouchure in the playing of wind instruments is related to proper breathing practices. Good tone quality is attained when the conductor knows how to correct faulty breathing practices.

Secondly, as in singing, it is important to practice how to sustain tones. In the development of a good sound on a wind instrument, or a stringed instrument, learning to produce a steady flow of tone should come before tongue, finger, and bow dexterity. Any student can learn to hit notes and run. Pressuring students into speedy note-chasing before a sustained tone is achieved can only be harmful. In the strings, the development of slow, sustained bow control is important from the very beginning. There is little to be gained from a clumsy attempt at dexterity before pupils are prepared for clearly articulated passages.

Aptitude and Coordination for Playing an Instrument

Thirdly, the instrumental teacher has a special responsibility to see that the pupil has an aptitude for the instrument which he chooses. Sometimes this is a matter of interest; at other times it may be a problem of poor coordination. A violinist must be able to place the right bow arm in proper relation with the moving fingers of the left hand, and at the same time involve the whole body in the feeling of the musical pulse.

The involvement of the hearing process in the production of the tone is of great importance. The production of a good tone on the violin requires a special kind of muscular, aural, and cerebral coordination. It might be better for some students to play a brass or percussion instrument. Each instrument requires a different kind of dexterity and coordination. The well-equipped teacher, one who can analyze the abilities of his students and is aware of the technical demands of all of the instruments, will direct them to the instruments with which they can function best.

Choosing and Keeping an Instrument in Proper Playing Condition

A serious factor in the development of the tone, of course, is the quality of the instrument on which the pupil plays. It is impossible to produce a beautiful sound on many of the instruments on which students perform. As soon as a learner is progressing well it is wise to encourage the parent to purchase a better instrument. Teachers can often use a collection of instruments which have been accumulated by the school, and which are available for lending to students, even though some of these are not of the finest quality. An orchestra which uses the poorest of instruments cannot, obviously, produce a fine singing tone. The teacher, however, can often find defects in instruments which can be repaired to improve the tone. A bow which has lost most of its hair, or one which has too much rosin after years of use, can be fixed to function more effectively. Extension tubing which is stuck on a brass instrument can be loosened so that the instrument can be tuned correctly. Felt pads which have become loose can be replaced to enable woodwinds to be played with better results. The careful selection of reeds cannot be emphasized too strongly. The replacement of the mouthpiece can often substantially improve the sound of a trumpet or a clarinet. The choice of the mouthpiece which suits the individual player is important. The teacher who has a knowledge of all factors which affect the tone is in a position to improve the quality of the sound in the ensemble.

The Importance of Developing Good Intonation

There are those who believe that perfect intonation in a high school orchestra is impossible. This may be true. Good intonation, however, is not impossible, as many groups throughout the country have already proven. It is certainly agreed that fine instrumental conductors must concern themselves with the problem and a part of all rehearsals should be devoted to it.

A number of elements contribute to the production of good intonation in an orchestra or band. First, a tuning guide for each instrument, kept in the folder at each stand, can be helpful in that it indicates to the student how to adjust a mouthpiece or a valve in order to achieve better intonation. In tuning an ensemble in the practice room it is probably best to use a tuning bar, A for the orchestra and Bb for the band. The oboe, which is most often used for the tuning of professional orchestras, is not as reliable for the average high school group, for it is capable of pitch variations. Here, the director uses his own best schooled judgment. The tuning bar has proven to be more helpful in amateur groups.

Second, good intonation on stringed instruments is, at best, difficult. The knowledgeable conductor knows that sometimes a revised set of fingerings will help the intonation. In playing a wind instrument, performers become aware of a number of devices for playing and altering the tone. There are times when skips from one position to another are clumsy and poor intonation results. Sometimes a slide trombone player can produce a tone better in pitch by using the fourth position instead of the first. This is also true in the case of the violin. A knowledge of the various positions can help to solve the problem.

Third, as in singing, a tone produced on a wind instrument with good breath support will help the performer to develop a controlled tone. With the strings this is infinitely more difficult. The string player must create each tone. The coordination between ear and fingers must help to determine where each finger falls on the fingerboard. Good intonation, of course, comes with continued practice in which the aural and tactile senses are coordinated.

Fourth, tuning the orchestra and the individual instruments to A or Bb has led to an improper concept of its function. The conductor must make his players aware of the importance of tuning the whole instrument. Tuning the ensemble, and each instrument in it, can best be accomplished through the use of unison scales. Here it is important that students learn to play in tune together. Some adjustment in the tuning of each instrument will be required. It is a wise conductor who chooses some pieces which have unison passages, or sections which deal with octaves or perfect fifths. Pulling these problems out of the score for exercise and drill will improve the intonation of the group, and the entire composition will be played better in pitch.

Fifth, loud playing interferes with the production of good intonation. Forcing the tone distorts the pitch, and when the music is loud it is difficult to hear poor intonation. It is good for the conductor to practice extractions from the score which is being rehearsed, and to drill on these sections more softly than the score indicates. When placed back in the music, in their proper context, these sections will tend to be played without flatting.

Sixth, the vibrato, in string playing, often disguises the production of improper pitches on the fingerboard. Temporarily dropping the vibrato can make the player more aware of intonation. Again, in involving the aural and tactile senses the pitches can be adjusted and the vibrato can be restored to beautify the tone.

Seventh, extremely high tones produced on the woodwind and brass instruments are often difficult to produce in pitch. The proper embouchure and support of the tone with air are important factors. In sectional rehearsals it is not hard to find those students who have better intonation and to place them at the proper stands where they can lead and motivate the others.

Balance and Intonation

There are a variety of technics and devices which the conductor uses to stress and improve intonation. Obviously, these accomplishments take time, organization, and drill. Students must be taught to listen actively. Each player must fit into a scheme of belonging because each part is important to the whole texture of the music. Only the conductor who studies the score in its entirety can determine where the music is out of balance, where one melodic line must sing out, and where another must be subdued. Good players must be placed in all of the parts. A mediocre second violin player does not help the overall sound of the orchestra. A good violinist in the second violin section helps to improve the sound.

The best balance in an orchestra or band will come if each section is balanced in itself. As each section becomes more proficient it can be combined with the others. The string section tends to dominate the orchestra. Brass and double reed instruments tend to cut through the whole texture of the orchestration. Players in an ensemble must be trained to develop greater controls so that they do not throw the balance in the group out of focus. In the rehearsals an ensemble must learn to follow the signals which a conductor sends out to indicate balance, tempi, and dynamics. These efforts can only result in greater balance within the group.

The Concertmaster and First Chair Positions

Choosing the section leaders or the concertmaster is often a problem. Some directors feel that it is more important to distribute the good players among the less skilled in order to motivate the pupils for better pitch production and higher skill standards. Others feel that each violinist or clarinetist should be given the opportunity and responsibility of playing from the first chair. Still others set up competitive tests to determine who will be in the first chair for the next year. Whatever the conductor decides to do should be determined by his desire to raise the skill level, the efficiency of the rehearsal, and the morale of the entire group.

Seating Plans for Orchestras of Various Sizes

In high school ensembles, especially those schools where a new instrumental program is being inaugurated, a balanced group is not always available. The conductor must use his own knowledge and skill to arrange a seating plan. Keeping in mind the objective of developing a balanced, coordinated, and beautiful sound, directors over the years have developed

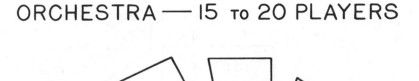

ORCHESTRA — 15 to 20 PLAYERS

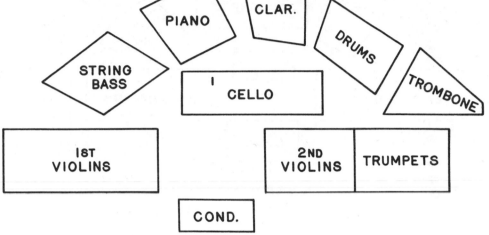

Figure 4–8

what are now traditional arrangements. There is nothing sacred about these listed here. Variations of these plans have been used from time to time with great success. The diagrams shown are but a few of those which are acceptable among music educators today.

The generally accepted seating forms should be used for a balanced sound. If the group is small a freer plan of organization might be contrived. A rearrangement of any of these seating plans may be desirable in order to achieve a better balance of tone. Today, with many different kinds of baffles, bandshells, and other acoustical aids, better instrumental combinations can be used. The positions of the various instrumental groups may vary, also, depending upon the balance needed for a particular selection or specific program, or on the size of the group, the pit, or the stage.

Handling Discipline Problems

The conductor of a high school instrumental ensemble deals with normal adolescents. From time to time discipline problems appear which

ORCHESTRA — 20 to 30 PLAYERS

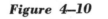

Figure 4–9

Figure 4–10

ORCHESTRA — 50 to 75 PLAYERS

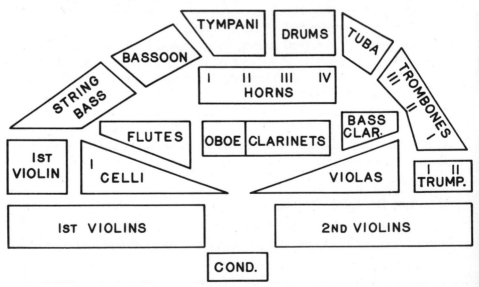

LARGE SYMPHONY ORCHESTRA

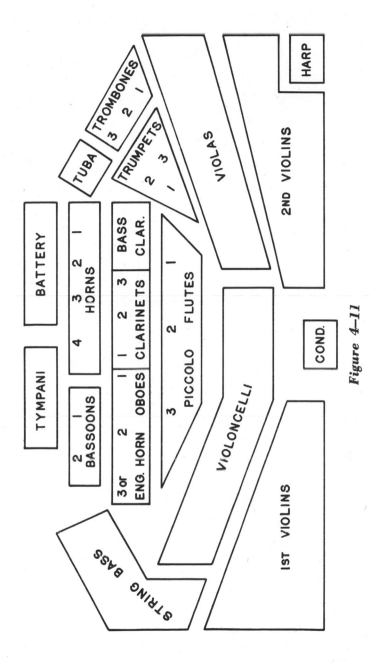

Figure 4-11

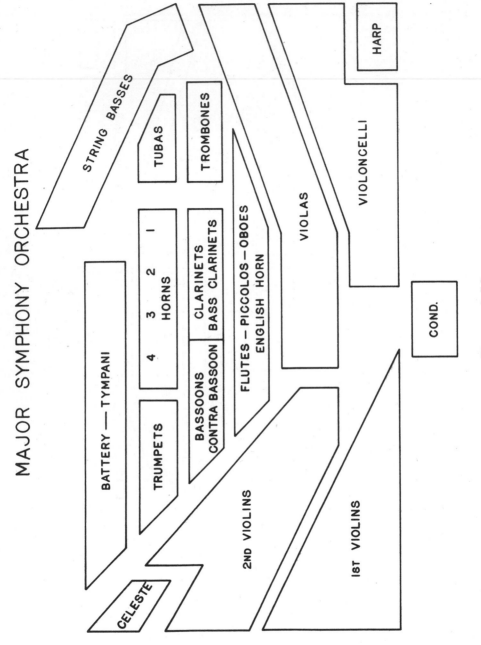

MAJOR SYMPHONY ORCHESTRA

Figure 4–12

he must be prepared to handle. Serious tasks, such as the study of master works for orchestra, demand built-in self-controls. The director who can develop a self-disciplined group is in a better position to do superior work than one who must superimpose rigid rules on the group. The practice of keeping all students busy in the study and performance of music which they find exciting is a healthy approach to the problem. The conductor has every right to expect complete and undivided attention when he comes before the group. The excitement and enthusiasm with which he makes the rehearsals interesting will help to build the necessary morale.

There are positive factors which work in favor of self-discipline. First, there are the normal group pressures which motivate individual members to excel. Second, the concerted group effort psychologically channels each player into the spirit of belonging. The conductor capitalizes on this. Commendation and praise, when deserved, help to motivate pupils who sense progress and achievement. The use of exciting and attractive music can create the atmosphere in which interest grows. Practice periods of serious study, alternated with good-humored light periods, tend to break tensions which sometimes build up.

In music education we are primarily interested in achieving the best musical results within the framework of broad educational objectives. This requires the self-discipline which develops when students recognize that they can make the best music when they work together in concert. First, the group must respect the conductor; second, the group members must have respect for their own abilities and the skills of their fellow performers. Simple rules and regulations should be strictly enforced but handled fairly. Attendance, punctuality, and self-discipline can be best achieved when group morale is high. Disciplines cannot be superimposed on a group; rather, each individual must discipline himself. There are times, of course, when the conductor must exercise his right as a teacher to bring a poorly disciplined individual into line with the objectives of the group. When the orchestra is immersed in an exciting rehearsal, the sheer pressures of the group activity will hold most individuals in line.

Some disciplinary problems arise from poor planning and an ill-advised choice of materials. At times, music being rehearsed is not much of a challenge, or is mediocre to the point of dreariness. The director can head off this kind of problem by not using it in the first place or by changing it as soon as possible. Music educators try to develop discriminating tastes in their students by means of competent instruction and guidance.

Planning Musical Programs

Program planning should reveal consideration for the instrumental ensemble which is performing and the audience which comes to hear it. Selections listed should be arranged for balance and coherence. Contrasting a composition in which the strings are featured with one in which the brasses and woodwinds stand out might be desirable. Above all, the sequence and arrangement of the pieces should make for a vibrant and exciting experience. In these days of the sound film, television, and UHF radio, children hear much sophisticated music. Their tastes are being influenced all of the time. Clever planning is important if the musical organizations are to be shown off to best advantage and enhance the musical taste of pupils throughout the school.

A symphony orchestra in a senior high school has much to be said in its favor. Its success is the result of an accumulation of technics developed over a period of years by many teachers, of building on long established traditions, and the introduction of new, effective procedures. All in all, the entire field of music education is to be commended for outstanding accomplishments in the field.

Popular Music in the Instrumental Program

School instrumental programs include all kinds of popular and folk music. Whether we call it rock, or soul music, or just popular music does not matter. Teachers encourage such activities as dance, rock and roll and stage bands, cowboy and country style bands, folk guitar, banjo, and other plectrum groups. Students with such interests should be encouraged to experiment with sound and through the experience should be taught to evaluate and improve their musicianship. Throughout the ages amateurs and professionals have played popular music. Many of them today make very exciting music without the help of the music teacher. With the help and guidance of an instructor they could produce an even better result. These activities should be a part of the instrumental curriculum, wherever they can be included, before school, during school or after school.

All instrumental activities can be used as avenues for musical growth. Usually, members of popular groups are also members of the school band or orchestra. Some members also want an opportunity to express themselves through the playing of popular music. The instrumental teacher who is skilled along these lines can make each activity a vital experience. The necessity for being skilled in rhythm can be pointed up very quickly. The need for a knowledge of transcribing, scoring for a small combo of instruments, learning of technics for precision playing, and developing a balanced tone, all can be made apparent by a watchful instructor. Pupils can be led to see that the rules for good musicianship apply here, also, if any success is to be achieved. Student conductors can be enlisted so that the teacher can be freed to move among the group members to see where the intonation needs improving, a rhythm or accent needs correction, or the balance needs adjusting so that a solo passage may be heard.

The instrumental teacher has a fine opportunity to mobilize all of his forces for the betterment of each individual and the entire school. The history of music education is a long story of individual and collective successes in introducing music to people. There are the pleasures of making music and the quiet joy of listening to it. Pupils who learn to make music must also learn to enjoy listening to it when it is performed. In training instrumentalists we should always keep in mind that growth and development are part of a continuous process. A good instrumental program helps each individual involved in it to grow at his own rate of speed, according to his own needs, and in the best interest of the group in which he plays.

Five

Stimulating

Musicianship

What is Musicianship?

Stated simply, musicianship is nothing more or less than the ability of a person to hear, see, picture and reproduce what the composer or creative artist has floating through his mind. A painter may be able to visualize, through the mind's eye, the line, form, and coloring of a painting either before it is painted, or "read it" after it is completed; but the musician who responds in a similar way must hear it first and through other senses see, feel and recreate it in his mind. In learning technical skills children progress from large and gross to small and refined manipulations. The learning process is helped along when the music is presented in a more artistic setting. The ability to picture, read, hear, and interpret; the ability to feel the tonal and rhythmic design emotionally; the ability eventually to recreate and reproduce—all these make one potentially more musical. Thus, a course in developing musicianship is a course in teaching students to hear and recreate music correctly.

When a student has acquired these abilities we can say that he is a musical person. When he plays a violin, sings, or plays the trombone, his technical ability may not be advanced but he will reveal an obvious musicality. How he turns a phrase, connects or disconnects the tones, shades a melodic line, will reveal the extent of his musicianship. All tests of musical ability or talent, if they do not test for this, do not test for musicianship, talent, or ability.

It is interesting to note, also, that developing musical ability in students heightens the excitement for technical advancement. When a pupil finds something important to say in music, he will more quickly find the means to say it, and that, after all, is what technics are all about. As a student goes from the crude, gross technical beginning, and develops a more refined proficiency and facility, what he has to say through a streamlined technic becomes more meaningful. A writer will refine his statement by placing his words in proper sequence; a musician will revise the order of his notes so that the message is more musical. The learner can study music theory, then, because he is directly concerned with the way in which notes relate to each other and express his musical ideas more clearly. Rules, of course, can be changed with the discovery of new technics and styles, for one does not learn or use theory by memorizing rules. One can only learn to utilize theory by developing a meaningful understanding of what is implicit in the rules.

Who Can Become Musical?

It is important to clear up the question of who can become musical. Some people would suggest that musicians are born because we find persons who are musical and others who obviously are not. In that case, why teach music at all and why have a music education program? Others feel that we can teach music up to a break-off point, beyond which one cannot go musically. Where, then, is this mysterious dot on the line of progress where talent ends and mediocrity begins? Music psychologists would be hard put to find the exact point at which one loses a responsiveness to music. We would like to maintain that there is no such point.

One needs no psychological testing to prove this thesis. At best, it can only reinforce what we already know: that people can respond in a musical way even if their technics are not well articulated. From the beginning of time, all people, in different parts of the world, under all kinds of conditions, regardless of race, nationality, or climate, age level or physical or mental maturity, have created music. By our standards some of these creations may be crude, but by their evaluations these might be quite sophisticated. The important observation to be made here is that much of it is exciting and overwhelmingly musical. Most of all, this tonal art has great meaning for the people who composed it. Obviously, then, the ability to respond to music is not a limited talent; it is a universal quality and there is little that is extraordinary about it.

Are we saying that everyone is a Schubert or a Mozart? Surely, that is not true. What we are suggesting is that there are differences in degree, conditioned by intelligence, by various human endowments, by the emotional responses of people, by an environment which is a potent factor, all of which effect the musicality of the pupil. Despite these limiting factors, all people can develop musicianship through which their lives can be enriched. This is the function of the educator and he must set up the music curriculum to meet the needs of people for expressing themselves in a musical way.

Implications for the Music Curriculum

After all of this has been said, what are the implications for the music curriculum? Surely, musicianship has to be taught in every course which springs up in the program. Musicianship is needed in the choir, the band, the orchestra; certainly, it is needed in all of the vocal and instrumental ensembles. It is not only important to show how a piece of music grows out of a specific scale; it is also important to show why a composer turns a phrase in a particular way in order to get across a musical idea. Perhaps the knowledge of the scale will help the sopranos of the choir to articulate a phrase better, or the jump of a major seventh in a passage for the basses may be sung better in pitch if the group sees that it comes right out of the major scale. Most technical difficulties are overcome by an awareness that the problem is usually a musical one. The development of musical awareness is an important part of music education. The extent to which the teachers of all music activities emphasize this awareness will determine the degree of musicianship which results.

Recently, a general music class was rehearsing a piece of music in a minor key which involved the production of a major third. The teacher was well aware of the flatting everytime the students came to a repeat of the interval.

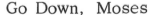

Figure 5–1

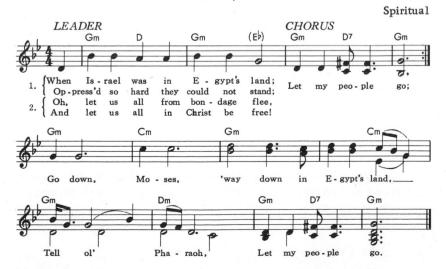

The teacher tried to have the class sing the song on a neutral syllable and the flatting persisted. The class was then asked to listen to the teacher sing it, to no avail. The group listened to the interval on the piano, and several members of the group who sang the passage correctly were asked to demonstrate it. The students repeated the sounds correctly, but on the repeat of the entire song the group reverted to singing:

Figure 5–2

When the teacher decided to take the song apart, briefly, to show how this musical phrase grows out of the melodic minor scale, the class got the point immediately. The students sang the ascending melodic minor scale.

Figure 5–3

The class drilled for a few moments on the related sounds of the scale. A drill on the upper tetrachord then followed. The fifth degree of the scale was then sung twice, the sixth degree was omitted, and the group went directly to singing the seventh degree twice and the eighth degree once.

Mi	Mi	Si	Si	La
Loo	Loo	Loo	Loo	Loo
Leht	*Mah-ee*	*Pee*	*Puh-l*	*Guh-oo*

Figure 5–4

The class understood the relationship immediately. Much time could have been saved in treating the problem as a musical one. Children must be taught to hear how it sounds and also to see how it came to be what it is. When we put the solved problem back into its proper context it becomes more meaningful.

Flatting and sharping on an instrument can be treated in precisely the same way. A string player has to hear the tone before he plays it and he must hear it in its proper context. The pianist and the xylophone player have no such problem. If their instruments are in tune they have no difficulties with pitch. The best way to overcome a musical problem, then, is to go to the music itself. What did the composer intend? If there is a basic rhythmic problem we must go to the rhythmic pattern. The individual notes, no matter how important, must not be allowed to get in the way, but can be learned later. Tapping out the beats first, their accents, then hanging the notes in the basic pattern on the beats will help. Counting out the rhythm arithmetically is confusing. It is better to feel the rhythmic sequences as they are supported by a pulse. The teacher must isolate the problem, and treat it as a living response. When the students "get the feel of it," the passage can be placed back in its proper context where it can be refined and take on new meaning.

Basic Responses to Music

It is commonly accepted that a child's basic response to music is to rhythm and melody. Modern music psychologists have come to believe that more basic is the response to tone. Babies respond to crooning and to all kinds of sounds around them. Surely we want to encourage children to respond to rhythm, to melody, and to the many sophisticated variations of sound which are sometimes foreign to them. The important matter here is that children can become responsive, from the beginning, to the imitation and production of beautiful tone. This is one of the reasons why a string teacher organizes drills and pieces which involve long, sustained tones almost from the beginning of study. Improving the tone quality of singers and instrumentalists is related to musicianship. Various tone qualities are used as a means of expressing one's self musically. Through changes in tone quality one can capture emotions, moods, and various shades of meanings. If tone is basic, then, an important part of the training for musicianship centers around tone production.

Musicianship Comes from Studying the Music

In a voice class, if a difficult technical passage is muddled and the singing insecure, it is best to isolate the section which is troublesome and to look to the music for the solution. An analysis of the passage can lead to an exercise in breathing, singing the florid notes in staccato style to eliminate smearing, and then quickly restoring the legato which the composer intended. In a choir rehearsal of the "Requiem Aeternam" from the Verdi *Requiem* the soprano soloist is required to sing a descant above the singing of the four-part chorus. The passage is sung a cappella. In many professional choruses it is not unusual to hear sections of this music which go off pitch. In rehearsing this selection with a high school choir one finds that the notes in themselves are not difficult. The vocal range is certainly not too high or low, nor is the musical content difficult to grasp. In amateur groups, the place where the music falls down occurs in the middle section where Verdi suddenly shifts from Bb minor to Bb major on the words "Et lux perpetua luceat eis" (and let perpetual light shine down upon them). What a revelation there suddenly comes after the choir chants the words "Requiem Aeternam." After the continuous pleading, beseeching, imploring, there comes suddenly the ray of light and hope, and with it the new mood produced by the change of key. Verdi also provides here a change in the phrasing, a shifting of the accents, and a transition from short, almost jerky, staccato-like snatches of phrases to a longer, slower, and sustained passage which captures the meaning of the words. Failure to go to the music for an interpretation can only lead to problems in getting the music across to the listener. Where to breathe, where to sigh, where to sustain, where to support the longer phrases all are dictated in the score. Every marking is important. The rests in the various voices are clearly indicated to suggest ends of phrases, places to breathe, and other places to prepare for what is to come. Accents take on new meaning. The directions, with words such as *portate*, *ancora*, *morendo*, have significance. The choral conductor must go to the music if he would build musicianship. It is all there, and the amateur group can learn to read it and grasp its full meaning.

To counteract the flatting, which usually occurs, the director must go directly to the musical problem by contrasting the Bb minor and major scales. Singing both scales on a neutral syllable makes the choir more aurally sensitive to the difficulty. Surely, if the passage is taken out of the piece, drilled, and then placed back in proper context, it can be made to sound better in pitch. In using this procedure we do more than work on intonation. We are developing in choir members a broader understanding of what they are singing and, in a word, we are developing musicianship.

In highly developed creative music classes there are further opportunities to stimulate musicianship. In many senior high schools there are now opportunities to introduce theory, harmony, counterpoint, orchestration and instrumentation, composition, conducting, sight-singing, ear-training and all of the disciplines necessary for the development of musicianship. With the exception of highly specialized situations, however, it is virtually impossible to set up these specialties as separate units. In most cases, where a special course in musicianship exists, it is set up

Figure 5–5: Excerpt from Verdi's Requiem

as "The Essentials of Music," "Music Theory," "Harmony," "Creative Music," or some other title which tries to suggest a conglomerate of musical activities all taught together in one classroom at the same time. The music teacher, therefore, in order to make the best use of the time, must organize the work so that maximum benefits can accrue to the students.

Creative Music Classes

There is another limiting factor—that of students who come to the class with some previous training while others come with more limited backgrounds. It is obvious that if the class is divided into different levels some organization is necessary to keep each working group at its own stage of development and each individual student progressing at his own rate of speed. While complicated, this is not an impossible situation. There are times when it may be necessary for the teacher to work with one, two, or three students at a time. There are other times when the teacher must work with all of the students at one time. Class times should be used flexibly to take care of individual needs, also, and time should be allotted in each session to clear up immediate problems.

Dividing the Class into Working Units

In order to organize the group for teaching, we must differentiate between the class which is divided into smaller units that allow for individual teaching levels and those activities which are conducted for the the group as a whole in order to train for broader musical objectives.

Smaller Units—Individual Teaching Levels

Theory I—Signs, symbols, nomenclature, clefs, notes, rests, scales
Theory II—Intervals, triads, chords, cadences
Harmony I—I, IV, V, V7, V9; four-part harmonizations; non-chordal tones; creative work
Harmony II—Primary and secondary chords; creative work
Harmony III—Modulation and counterpoint; creative work
Harmony IV—Form; composition

Activities for the Whole Class—Broader Objectives

Sight singing
Rhythmic drills
Ear training
Dictation
Listening lessons
Form and analysis
Orchestration and instrumentation
Melody writing
Conducting
Individual and group performances; auditions
Creative work on all levels; new trends in harmony and composition.

At the beginning of the year a survey should be made by the teacher to determine the level of musical development for each individual student. After diagnostic tests and auditions, it may be found that students can be placed in two categories:

LEVELS OF INSTRUCTION		INSTRUMENTAL SKILLS	
Students	Subject	Students	Skill
6	Theory I	7	Piano
4	Theory II	3	Violin
5	Harmony I	4	Trumpet
3	Harmony II	4	Clarinet
3	Harmony III	1	Violoncello
1	Composition and	2	Percussion
	creative work	1	String bass
22		22	

Setting Up a Rotating System for Unit Teaching

A good way to keep the entire class working at the same time is to institute a unit system with assignments of work due on a given day of each week. A minimum of one unit is due as home work, but any student can progress at his own rate of speed and turn in as many units as he is able to complete effectively. The instructor teaches each small unit separately at whatever level the group finds itself. For example, while three students are being taught the subject matter of Unit 8 in Harmony II, the remainder of the class will be working independently at their desks. When the teacher is finished teaching one small group, he moves around the room answering questions for those pupils who need help. After several days in which the teacher has given instruction to all unit groups, the entire class for one or two sessions may begin to work on some rhythmic drills or sight singing in one, two, three, or four parts. The entire year's work can be outlined to include all subject matter necessary for the development of musicality in a given area.

Programming Units of Work

A unit system which the theory and harmony class can use is not always available in a published text. Within the last few years some books for high school students have been published in the field of theory but very little is available for the teaching of harmony by a unit system. The teacher can prepare a series of units which can be studied and completed as homework by pupils. As each student arrives at new materials, lessons may be taught which anticipate the problems. There are times when a student, moving at his own rate of speed, comes upon difficulties which he cannot solve himself. As the teacher walks among the group members he can give the necessary help so that the pupil does not become frustrated. Where teaching machines are available some of this work can be programmed for student use.

Hearing the Music

Musical problems of a general nature will come up with regularity. Care should be taken that the element of hearing is not minimized. It is important at every stage of development that whatever is taught or written by the students *must be heard.* If the students are being taught the subject matter of intervals or triads, the approach should be aural. As many devices and illustrations as possible must be given at the piano or on recordings. If there is a four-part harmonization completed on the blackboard it should be sung in parts, with syllables, numbers, or a neutral syllable. If in an audition the pupil plays a Mozart Sonata, the class and the teacher together should analyze the form and learn to recognize it aurally. If a difficult rhythmic problem presents itself, a drill can be set up for the entire class so that all can benefit from the experience. The hearing of the harmonies and the rhythms should be of paramount importance.

Where there are practice rooms, of course, students may be permitted to use the pianos to test harmonizations and other work. The emphasis on hearing should always prevail. Ear-training drills should be organized in terms of the scale, intervals, and triads. Melody writing, identification, and dictation are other ways in which to develop the ability to hear. Music is an aural art and the theory and harmony class should never deteriorate into a place where exercises are given in mechanical writing. A completed exercise should always be discussed by the class with an eye and ear for making it more musical. The introduction of non-chordal tones, embellishments, and other dissonances can help to make the simplest harmonizations more interesting and more musical to hear.

Modern Trends in Harmony

Students should be lead into the realm of good taste, however. The use of dissonance and modern devices should be limited only by what the pupils have to say in music. Much of this teaching can lead to the rules which have evolved over centuries of music writing. Here, the teacher may bring in new trends in harmony and creative composition. What did Schoenberg and Berg contribute that is new? What about serial music? Electronic music? What about dissonance in general? Students should be encouraged to bring in newspaper clippings, programs, and program notes written for concerts. Discussions which grow out of these activities should whet the appetites of pupils for exploring new ideas in creative music.

Relevance and Function of Creative Work

Relevance and function are important. Recently in a creative music class a pupil who plays the piano and organ and sings well was trying to compose a piece for the piano. While able to improvise the most intricate harmonies and progressions at the piano, his piece was in the eclectic style of Haydn, Mozart, and Beethoven. It reflected a knowledge of 18th century styles. The boy was of black heritage, active in the black student circles, and keenly aware of the struggle of the Negro in our society. The music which he was writing was hardly relevant, functional, or interesting. When he played preliminary sketches of his piece in class for criticism, the discussion centered around what style of music would apply for our times and what style of music would best reflect the boy's own environment and concerns. How can a composer function in our society? was also asked. Slowly there began to evolve the feeling that his original music should reflect his heritage. How is this done? How did the composers of the past do it? Aaron Copland, George Gershwin, William Grant Still, how did they do it? Recordings were brought into class; analyses were made. Form, structure, germs of musical ideas borrowed from the environment, the development of germs into motives, themes, melodies, and compositions—all these were demonstrated. A whole new world of ideas was opened up for the students. What was the heritage that this student-composer could draw upon? The class began to list them: the blues; spirituals; Jubilee songs; barrelhouse; boogie-woogie; the cakewalk; the shuffle; African rhythms, melodies, and instruments; Afro-Cuban songs and dances; the blues note in jazz; the various individual rhythms and melodic contrasts from African countries such as Angola, Kenya, and Southern Rhodesia; Haitian drum rhythms; Afro-American rhythms found in such dances as the Conga, the Samba, the Merengue, the Juba, and in the Creole music of Louisiana.

The student-composer came to see that all about him in his environment he could find the germs of musical ideas for writing music which were of his time and moment and which had relevancy for him. His first piece was a Bb tenor saxophone solo, with piano accompaniment, a hauntingly naive piece which he called "Interlude." In listening to the music, no one could mistake the sound of the black influence. Composing the music gave the student a sense of pride, a feeling of accomplishment and worth. In the process, the young man had to learn how to record on paper the form and structure, the content and substance of his ideas, the signs and symbols through which any interpreter could grasp what he had in mind when he composed the music. In writing the solo for the Bb tenor saxophone the composer had to learn about its range, its various tone qualities, and its limitations. Thus, composing set up the machinery for a music-growth which pushed the student far ahead of his group. The class, also, benefitted from the experiences and others began to experiment with musical ideas ripe for development.

There is some doubt that this boy and his classmates will become composers by profession. The musical values of these creative experiences, however, cannot be questioned. Relevancy is important and any composer of worth must face it, if for no other reason than that the music must be relevant to the composer himself. If, in addition, it is functional and useful to others, then it can take on additional meanings. Certainly, as a learning experience, it can help to accomplish all of the objectives of a course in creative writing. In the process of writing, the pupil develops the kind of musicianship through which he can constructively evaluate a growth process. One need not be a Beethoven to appreciate a Beethoven, but one can appreciate Beethoven more when he becomes aware of the skills and technics which make the composer great.

Practical uses of music should be encouraged. Writing in small forms is always desirable for novices. Popular songs, folk-type songs, those with or without a direct message, and art songs are a good starting point. When instrumentation and orchestration are taught, arrangements for jazz combo should be encouraged. Students should develop a knowledge of old and new instrumental styles, with an understanding of contemporary trends. Small, refined forms, such as string trios or quartets, are more difficult to compose. Writing small, cameo-like pieces requires a special approach. With high school students the approach should always be practical and functional.

Electing a Creative Music Course

In those schools where the theory and harmony class, or the creative music class is given as a separate subject, it should be compulsory for those students who have enrolled in the music major curriculum. These students can get an early start in musicianship training before entering a college or conservatory. Others, those not tending to specialize, should be given an opportunity to elect the course. This class will provide amateurs with the necessary background for greater musicality and enjoyment. Full major credit should be provided for those who elect this specialty.

To summarize, we develop musicianship by permitting pupils to work with music materials under guidance, encouraging the process of seeing, hearing, and picturing music. All of the technics and manipulations, from gross to refined, can be acquired when the motivations for deeper insights and meanings become apparent. The heightened excitement and the growing love of music can lead to a proficiency, skill, and depth of understanding which we call musicianship.

Six

Teaching Music
Appreciation and
Music Literature

Teaching requires good salesmanship, and most pupils can be taught if we organize for the sales campaign. The teacher, like the salesman, must constantly be aware of student interest and know when and how to change the approach and add new materials which will be of value. Enthusiasm is an integral part of the salesman's bag of tricks. Like the measles, it is contagious and must be caught. The initial stages are of primary importance. Maintaining an enthusiasm for music, however, requires much more than an emotional approach. The music teacher has the responsibility of providing the kinds of contacts with music which are more lasting.

Meaning, Relevance and Identification

Ideally, exposure to music which leads to appreciation should occur throughout the music curriculum. It is the aim of the choral and instrumental teacher to teach appreciation through the manipulations which are necessary for performance. Everyone is aware of the depth of feeling and understanding which can come from direct contact with music-making. Music teachers also know that many pupils make music without feeling, understanding, or appreciating it. What is it, then, that makes the difference? Surely the answer is related to what one may call meaning, relevance, and identification.

Some students cannot, will not, or have no desire to make music. All, however, can learn to listen actively and participate through an aural approach to appreciation. Young people listen to a variety of popular and folk music which is relevant to them. Many go beyond this to enjoy favorite concert selections passively. The music teacher who can take pupils from this point to new experiences in listening serves a very important function in their lives. A whole new world is opened for those who can find relevancy in a wider spectrum of musical offerings.

Understanding What Makes a Piece of Music Great

Young people want to know, however, why it is that popular music is so exciting that they want to jump to it, whereas much of the concert music leaves them cold on a first hearing. To them, it is the excitement which makes for greatness in music. Novices in the field of music listening may find it difficult to adjust immediately to the concert medium. This frequently leads to the question of what makes the music of one composer great and that of another not so great. If we can answer this question for our young people, we can come closer to teaching music appreciation more effectively. Surely, we say, a Rubin Goldmark or a Johann Stamitz was recognized in his own time as great, only to be relegated to oblivion in subsequent generations. These men were recognized as great by their own peers. We come to see, then, that sophistication in music writing, without substance and meaning, does not lead to identification. The music of Josef Haydn, removed from our generation by over 200 years, is more relevant and meaningful to us today than the music of Rubin Goldmark who is chronologically much closer to us.

Music, Emotions, and Communications

Music appreciation, of course, has something to do with emotions, ideas, ideals, man's aspirations, fundamental philosophies, and the mysteries of life. Those men who use the technical knowledge and facilities to transmit, communicate, and capture fundamental human emotions so that future generations can identify with them can be called great. Men like Shakespeare, Rembrandt, and Bach are great not only because they had great facility, but also because they expounded and transmitted universal truths which are just as meaningful today as they were in their own time.

Two Approaches to Appreciation

How does one make this idea relevant to high school students? There are two approaches to appreciation: one is emotional, the second is intellectual. First we feel through our emotions; then we intellectualize what we feel. High school students can understand this. What are some of the fundamental human emotions that all of us have experienced, we ask them. Can we list them? Joy, sorrow, fear, hate, anger, exhilaration, happiness, despair, resignation, love are but a few that students can name. Let us hear a piece of music now, with no title, no name of composer, no indication of who is playing the music. The teacher plays the prelude to the third act of *Lohengrin* by Richard Wagner. The class jumps with excitement. Now listen to this one—the teacher plays an orchestral transcription of *Come Sweet Death* by Johann Sebastian Bach. Without any previous knowledge of what the composer intended, students cannot help but see that both composers captured fundamental human emotions in these compositions. What did the class members feel in contrasting both pieces? Then, what did the composer intend to transmit and communicate to the listener? Slowly, as judgments are refined, as pupils begin to study and listen thoughtfully, they come to see and hear what the composer really had in mind. There are, of course, many compositions which have no such titles. These are, however, no less real in emotional and intellectual content. Each listener, if he chooses to do so, can read himself into the music and identify with it.

What, then, is the conclusion about learning to appreciate? Simply stated, so that every student can get the point, is the deduction that first, anybody can learn to "jump" to music of one kind or another, without knowing anything about it, and second, when we learn why and how we come to appreciate it, the process becomes more meaningful. There are choices to be made, and as we learn more about music our choices change. This brings about an awareness of the power of music. It also presents the necessity for students to be exposed to many different kinds of music, performed by a variety of fine musicians. Pupils can learn to identify with a wide cross section of the world's culture, developing along the way keen insights and skills for listening.

In many music appreciation classes great emphasis is placed on theme recognition. In all fairness to the composer, and the listener who is often more limited, the important thing is to see what the composer did with the theme. When George Frederick Handel was accused of stealing a melody from one of his peers, he said flatly: "That pig doesn't know what to do with such a tune!" Sometimes a creative artist states his theme in a simple way; but a Milton, a Daumier, or a Mozart not only states his idea but also comments on it. What he has to say about the theme is often more important than the theme itself. Students can come to see that each composer, in tackling universal ideas, makes his contribution to our great cultural wealth in his own inimitable way.

Popular and Folk Music

The teacher can develop better rapport with his students if he is more understanding of the popular music which is enjoyed by so many young people. Dance music and popular ballads have always been an important part of music history. There are many available examples which show that composers idealized these forms in serious compositions. Many music educators, in looking back at their own adolescence, remember playing in dance bands, singing popular songs of the day, and dancing the latest steps on the dance floor. Most of them managed to survive the ordeal. Most of them developed an interest in music from these exciting beginnings in the popular culture.

Popular songs and dances have their place in present-day culture, as they have had in all preceding cultures. Our problem is one of keeping up with new developments and trying to understand them. It is not fair to expect high school students to live in the past. Also, we cannot live in their world, but as teachers we must find a way to communicate with them. A knowledge of current popular music can be revealing and can help us to understand these very live pupils who sit in our classrooms. It can also lead us to some sophisticated germs of musical ideas which will eventually find their way into our art forms. Jazz, which was the popular music of the twenties, has already done this. It is safe to say that contributions which are being made today will ultimately appear in our serious music. Most important is the feeling of students that a music teacher who understands the culture of the past, as well as that of the present, is one who looks to the future.

Organizing for the Teaching of Subject Matter

Now that we have said all this, how do we begin a course in music appreciation? There are a number of avenues for attack. The traditional one, that of presenting chronologically a series of musical compositions for study, is least effective and we will dispose of it first. The argument given in its favor is that it organizes the learning process for the students, but nothing could be further from the truth. This procedure only organizes the materials in what is called a "logical" sequence; it does not organize the learning process. Part of this approach stems from the desire to teach subject matter. Antagonism to teaching subject matter stems from a failure of the teacher to realize its importance. Properly understood, the teaching of subject matter is important in the development of the individual. Learning how to read and write and handle numbers is important, and failure to learn to perform in these areas is an indication that the teacher as the organizer of the learning has also failed. The teacher must release the energies of the pupils to make it possible for them to function and to learn. In working with the group, he can arrive at subject matter for discussion, recommend books to read, prepare for checking through tests to see how much has been transmitted and absorbed, and suggest materials which are needed by students for further growth and development. In the light of these conclusions, the chronological approach is the least desirable. There may be teachers, however, who can carry it off to a good start. If we begin with the music of Bach and his predecessors, and include all of the music up to electronic music, we find that there is too much material to cover. Limitations of time make it imperative that much important material be eliminated. We should not aim to cover ground. Our emphasis should be on quality, attitudes, and understandings.

In teaching it is always best to go to the core of the problem and face the class with the question: "How does one learn to appreciate music?" Let's not beat around the bush, it suggests. If there are two approaches to the teaching of appreciation, the emotional and the intellectual, teachers and students must explore them together.

First, with the emotional approach, pupils can get to hear and like such compositions as:

1812 Overture—Tchaikovsky (emotions connected with war)
Aria: "Vesti La Giubba" from *Pagliacci*—Leoncavallo (despair)
Prelude to Act III from *Lohengrin*—Wagner (rejoicing)
Overture to the *Marriage of Figaro*—Mozart (set mood for comedy)
Come Sweet Death—Bach (grief)
Mad Scene from *Lucia Di Lammermoor*—Donizetti (joy and sadness)
Prelude to Act IV of *Traviata*—Verdi (sets mood for tragedy)

The Emotional Approach

Here, the group learns that on an emotional basis one need not analyze the music at all. These selections create the mood for depicting fundamental human emotions and one need not rationalize or intellectualize the music in the beginning. One of the objectives of the music teacher is the revelation of the relevancy of music in daily living. Playing the "Crucifixus," followed by the "Et Ressurexit, both from the *Mass in B Minor* by Johann Sebastian Bach, is a marvelous contrast between the moods of grief and exhilaration. Literally, this is painting in musical tone. Students can grasp this music immediately on an emotional basis.

The Intellectual Approach

The instructor teaches best when he utilizes the social set-up of the group. Directed discussion is a wonderful help in learning. Here opportunities present themselves for an interchange of knowledge, the presentation of new ideas, and the development of special interests. Many students enjoy talking about their interests and concerns. Good classroom discussions grow out of a central theme or focus. As they move on to the intellectualization of the music, students are willing to discuss their emotions freely. They quickly discover that all human beings experience the same emotions. They are fascinated to find how beautifully Richard Wagner depicted the emotion of love in the "Liebestod" from *Tristan and Isolde*. Adolescents who are just beginning to experience erotic emotions find the music of Wagner particularly moving. When, in addition, they see a typical page in the music score, with its many notes and notations, they are overwhelmed by the ability of a composer to record such feelings.

The teacher can capitalize on this and turn to other music which has captured erotic emotions. Art songs, blues songs, popular songs all can lead to dances, old and new, to boy-girl relationships in music, and the idealization of germs of these musical ideas in serious forms. This can lead to the Ländler of Schubert, the waltzes of the Strauss family, the waltz from the *Fifth Symphony* of Tchaikovsky, the cakewalk from the *Afro-American Symphony* of William Grant Still, and the American folk opera *Down in the Valley* by Kurt Weill. Gradually, we begin to intellectualize the folk forms. What can we find out about the composer? How does the world in which he lived relate to the music? What is the form? Would the class like to follow a skeleton score for the "Minuet" from *Symphony No. 40 in G Minor* by Mozart (Figure 6–1)?

The Developmental Approach

Using the developmental approach allows the students to make choices, to participate in the classroom decisions, and to decide for themselves what their preferences in music are. Musicians prefer many different kinds of music and their tastes are constantly changing. They should expect more not less from their students. Pupils must be allowed to change their minds as they grow in their preferences. The important thing here is the exposure to a large variety of music and a vast assortment of ideas about music. If we are educating for musical growth, teachers must allow their pupils to follow their own bent. It is a mistaken notion that children must like all of the music which they hear in school.

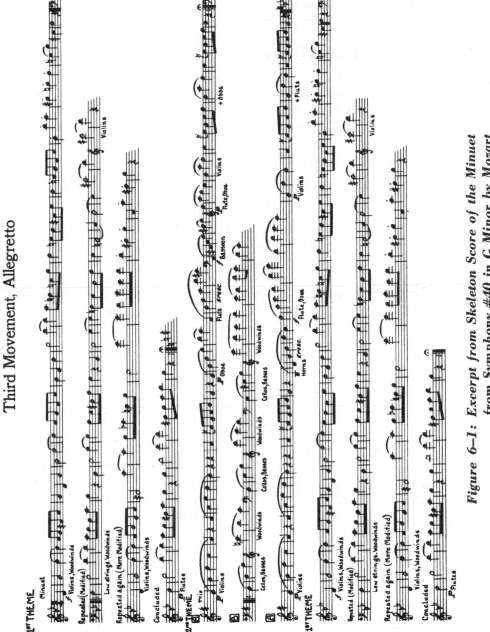

Figure 6–1: Excerpt from Skeleton Score of the Minuet from Symphony #40 in G Minor by Mozart

Students come to school to learn, among other things, how to make choices. We must not deny them the opportunity.

Utilizing the Concerns of Youth

Recently, a teacher in a ghetto school began to experiment with the idea of developing a music appreciation course which centered around the concerns of youth. He discussed the problems which young people face today and asked the class to list them. Foremost among them was war and how young people are affected by it. Boy-girl relationships came in a close second. On the list were placed such items as the generation gap, political and social justice, segregation and integration, the conflict between ideals and practicality, jobs and spending money, the desire to be loved, needed, and accepted by the society in which they lived, and how to face the future while striving to set goals for schooling and a profession or trade. All of these concerns were real, vital, and pressing.

This presented an opportunity for the class to learn that all of these emotions have existed in the past. Great composers have not only recorded them in music but have also commented on them. Students came easily to see that they are not alone with these deep inner feelings. At no time did the teacher sacrifice subject matter or content. Placed in this unusual context, the materials covered by the class took on broader and deeper meanings.

Concerns with War in Music

Students who were experiencing deep feelings with regard to war found it easy to identify with *Symphony No. 5* by Dmitri Shostakovich. One of the boys in the class brought in a recording entitled "Hitler's Inferno." This led to a classroom discussion which grew out of hearing the marching songs of the Hitler Youth. Hitlerian philosophy was identified with the music of Richard Wagner and particularly with the Ring Cycle. Soon the discussions turned to Fascist Italy, Mussolini and the highly nationalistic *Fountains of Rome* and *Pines of Rome* by Ottorino Respighi. American Civil War songs brought the class to the music of Charles Ives. *The 1812 Overture* of Tchaikovsky and the *Two Grenadiers* of Robert Schumann were linked to the Napoleonic Wars. The opera *Aida*, with its conflicting emotions related to the eternal triangle, brought the group to a war between Ethiopia and Egypt. *Andrea Chenier* by Giordano and the *Marseillaise* by De Lisle suggested a link with the French Revolution. The incidental music from *Egmont* by Beethoven revealed the struggle between the political and religious factions in the war between the Spanish and the Dutch. "The Rakoczy March" of Hector Berlioz presented a fiery scene from one of the Hungarian wars. The exciting *Third Symphony* (*Ilya Mourometz*) by Reinhold Glière drew upon ancient Russian history and mythology and described the war exploits of Svyatagor and Prince Vladamir. The *Hary Janos Suite* of Zoltan Kodaly introduced the class to the imaginary war experiences of Hungary's legendary liar. This unit of work included a study of the maps of Europe, poetry and literature, paintings and drawings, all related to the concerns of students about war.

Concern with Boy-Girl Relationships in Music

Musical selections which dealt with boy-girl relationships and sex were brought in with great ease. Popular, folk, concert, and operatic excerpts revealed a musical commentary on the erotic emotions of man. The "Liebestod" from *Tristan and Isolde* by Richard Wagner was contrasted with a modern folk-rock song which tries to depict the same emotion. Of the folk-rock selection, "Going Home," one student said, "You feel it more with your body." The Wagner excerpt, one student concluded, was more intellectual, "and it made you think about what your body was feeling." The class found the love duet from the end of the first act of *La Bohème* the most beautiful. They asked to have it repeated. The group enjoyed the slow movement from the *Symphonie Fantastique* of Hector Berlioz, where the composer states and comments on the theme of his "beloved." In the *Enigma Variations* by Sir Edward Elgar, the first variation describes the wife of the composer and reveals his love for her. The *Hary Janos Suite* includes an episode in which the hero conjures up for his friends a description of the beautiful girl, Orze; this braggart who breaks the hearts of all women, here boasts of his amoral exploits as the orchestra comments on the beauty of the woman. In the final scene from *Salomé*, by Richard Strauss, the depraved girl, who cannot have Johannan as a lover in life, chooses to make love to the bloody head which has been served to her on a silver platter. All of the disgust and revulsion are revealed in the music as Salomé caresses the head of Johannan, while repeating over and over again, "Ah, I have kissed your mouth, Johannan." The final scene from *Götterdämmerung*, by Richard Wagner, depicts Brunhilde riding into the funeral pyre of her husband and lover. It reveals another kind of idealized love, with an emphasis on eroticism, passion, and self-immolation. This scene, which recalls all of the motifs heard in the Ring Cycle, sums up Wagner's comments on love, hate, and greed. In contrast with this, the aria *Depuis le Jour* (Ever Since the Day) from the opera *Louise*, by Gustave Charpentier, has captured all of the sweet naivete of first love in Paris as experienced by a lovely little dressmaker. Adolescents can easily identify with the stirrings which they have already felt and can now recognize.

Many examples of the love emotion are depicted in music. High school students come to the classroom with a background gained from watching television, attending movies, and reading books. The high school music teacher is in an excellent position to serve a two-fold objective: first, to get pupils to think more objectively about their emotions; and second, through the process to make great musical masterpieces more meaningful.

Music and the Generation Gap

The generation gap came up for discussion in class and this too was illustrated by music and supplementary readings about the composers. Certainly, there were many composers who had to overcome the objections of parents to a musical career. Hector Berlioz' parents withdrew his allowance when he left his studies for the medical profession to prepare for a career in creative music. Tchaikovsky and Moussorgsky suffered similar parental objections. There are operatic stories which deal with other aspects of the generation gap. *Traviata, Louise, Gianni Schicchi, Lakmé, Rosencavalier, The Barber of Seville, The Bartered Bride, Die Meistersinger* all have stories with which young people can identify. It is interesting to note, also, that a number of composers who in their youth rebelled against existing rules set up by their elders, later became rigid themselves in teaching young students. Hector Berlioz, for example, unhappy with the rigidness of the past, rebelled against accepted standards of orchestration and wrote his own treatise on the subject. Then to his dying day he rigidly insisted that his disciples follow *his* precepts.

Music, Social Problems, and Politics

Music which deals with social and political problems is plentiful. The teacher here drew upon Beethoven's *Ninth Symphony, Tosca, Andrea Chenier, Boris Godounow, Don Carlos, Fidelio, Trial by Jury, Die Meistersinger, Till Eulenspiegel's Merry Pranks*, the "Marseillaise," *Billy the Kid*, the polonaises of Chopin, *Chester* by Billings, and *Peter and the Wolf* by Prokofieff. Many composers, in choosing subjects which deal with emotional themes, inject social and political ideas into individual scenes and comment musically on the ideas. Thus, in the opera *La Bohème* by Puccini there are several scenes in which the characters comment on the lot of the poor. In all of his operas, Guiseppe Verdi makes reference to some aspect of the social scene. Beethoven, even in his symphonies which have no words, presents the stirrings of the French Revolution and thereby comments on the great conflict of his times. Young people who are sensitive to their environment are quick to feel the emotions depicted in the music when they are presented in this light. A simple song like "The Battle Hymn of the Republic," with words by Julia Ward Howe, is one of our great social documents and should be presented as such.

Music and Identification

In their desire to be loved, needed, and accepted by the world in which they live, students can find solace in the stories of composers' lives and can identify with their music. Young people can identify with heroes, musical and otherwise. The Funeral March from the *Eroica Symphony* of Beethoven was just as significant at the funerals of the late John F. Kennedy and Martin Luther King as it was in the time of the composer. An understanding of love, need, and acceptance can be deepened by a study of music which reveals how a composer felt about these emotions. The resignation which Schubert feels in "Die Krähe" (The Raven) is fundamental. Pupils in this class were able to identify with the poet and the composer, both of whom were resigned to their fate.

Technical Music Materials

To what extent should the teacher of music appreciation use technical information, the reading of musical scores, the discussion of form and analysis? A great deal will depend upon the background which the students bring to the class. In many cases pupils have a limited background in music and find the technical approach to music awesome. The emotional approach, at the beginning, followed by an increasing amount of intellectualization is perhaps better. Whenever the need for technical information presents itself the teacher should inject it into the course. There are a number of interesting ways, for example, to introduce the various patterns, forms, and blueprints. How these are introduced is extremely important. Form should never be introduced for its own sake; it is important only in that it clarifies what the composer had to say.

In one music appreciation class, the teacher in teaching the sonata form placed the following outline on the blackboard:

The Logic of Form

```
Introduction
Statement:        1—theme ⎱
                  2—theme ⎰ Repeat
Development:      1—theme
                  2—theme
Recapitulation:    theme 1
                   theme 2
Coda
```

To explain the logic in this blue print he pointed to the local election for mayor of the city and showed how a campaign speech could be made utilizing the same form:

Introduction:
> Ladies and Gentlemen, I come before you today to discuss the issues of the campaign with the hope that you will support our party and its platform. I am running for mayor on the following platform:

Statement:
> 1. Lower taxes
> 2. A better water supply system
> Repeat: "And if I am elected, I promise to:
> (1) reduce the tax rate, and
> (2) produce a better water supply system."

Development:
> Ever since I was a boy I recall that almost every candidate for mayor has been promising relief from the pressures of increased taxes. As late as four years ago, when our present mayor campaigned for office, we were promised a revision in the tax structure of the city. To date, nothing has been done about the problem.
> With regard to the serious problem of water shortages and possible contamination, we must state that the present water supply system dates back to 1903 and is archaic. Since that time we have put many patches on it.
> The last survey which was made cost the taxpayers a quarter of a million dollars and showed that the present sources of water are no longer able to meet the needs of a growing city. New sources must be found.

Recapitulation:
> And so, in conclusion, I want to urge you to support our party and its platform. If we are elected in November we promise to bring you: (1) a long delayed revision in our tax structure, and (2) a much needed, modern water supply system.

Coda:
> I want to thank you for coming to hear us present the issues of the campaign, and urge you to support the whole slate on election day.

A simple device, such as this, not only ties up the music with daily living issues; it also helps to focus the attention of the students on the sonata form which is being studied. A painting or a piece of sculpture, which can be seen; a short story, a dress pattern, the recipe for a cake— all are related to forms in music. Balancing one phrase against another can be compared to the Gothic arch in architecture. The subject and predicate in grammar can be likened to a melody which also has a thesis and an antithesis. There are many ways in which the concept of form can be taught without getting too technical in the early stages of appreciation. The more that the teacher draws on the background and experience of the students, the better.

Preparing a Course of Study

Preparing and writing a course of study, before meeting the students, is easy enough, but making it relevant and meaningful is another matter. Experience has proven that, if the background of the teacher is a broad one, it should not be too difficult to develop a program of learning which evolves from the needs and interests of students. This does not necessarily mean that we must begin with jazz and develop a whole course which focuses around the history and development of our popular music. Jazz, as has already been stated, has its place in the curriculum. Some teachers, however, begin there and stay there. The end result is a limited program with a narrow series of musical experiences. It is much better to start with an attractive topic on which to focus the attention of the class and go on from there. Jazz excerpts can be brought in as another illustration of a point which the teacher is trying to make. If, for example, the class has been studying primitive rhythms, and has just heard the "Polovetsian Dances" from *Prince Igor* by Borodin, jazz rhythms can be brought in to show how a similar effect is created in American folk idioms. When teaching song form (A B A), there is no reason why the instructor cannot use a popular song and then show how Beethoven utilized the same form in the slow movement of the Pathétique Sonata. An evolving curriculum is not only more interesting for the pupils; it also presents a wider range of listening material.

The Teaching of Music Literature

The course in music literature is usually more advanced. Greater emphasis is placed on the masterpieces which are studied. A background related to music history, theory, score reading, form and analysis, musical instruments, the human voice, helps one to understand the performance of the literature better. With an emphasis on the music and its content, the focus is limited and less general. If we are studying the *First Symphony* of Johannes Brahms the work can be dissected and put together again. The themes can be presented and the organization which utilizes the themes can be clarified. Full or skeleton scores can be used so that the eye can see what the ear hears. Attention can be focused on the germs of musical ideas which are expanded and contracted as needed. The craftsmanship which the composer displays in his work is fascinating to watch, and is one of the aspects of his work which make the symphony exciting. Most of all, the monumental and lofty treatment of the themes, both in the statement and the development, makes this a great work of art.

There is a tendency in the teaching of music literature to present a survey course in which the material is already well organized. This method has little meaning for high school students. Since there is a lack of excitement in this approach, the teacher may not be able to supply enough stimulation to sustain interest. There is little opportunity for relieving the seriousness in a formal approach.

A more meaningful method for presenting materials is to compare similar works written in different eras and under different circumstances. For example, placing the *B. Minor Mass* of Johann Sebastian Bach side by side with the *Missa Criolla* of Ramirez, a folk mass from Argentina, or the *Missa Luba*, a folk mass from the Congo in Africa, can create exciting musical experiences. The teacher can compare the *Fifth Symphony* of Beethoven with the *Fifth Symphony* of Tchaikovsky, Shostakovich, Sibelius, Dvorák, Haydn (D Major—B and H 93), Mahler and Prokofieff. Not only can the form be analyzed but the styles of the different periods can also be compared.

Comparing the violin concertos of each period, classical, romantic and modern, may point up differences in style and content. The reading of background materials with regard to the period out of which the music grew can develop an understanding of styles. Piano concertos may be studied in a similar manner. Outlines of themes found in various symphonic forms may be posted on bulletin boards. Students can be encouraged to attend concerts in which these or similar works are played, to go to the school or public library where they can hear recordings again, and to build record collections of their own. The proof of success is in the desire of pupils to hear as much music as possible.

Modern to Classical Approach

Another sequence that may be used is one that begins with modern times and shows how our music came to be what it is. One could begin by using the *Concerto in F* of George Gershwin, go to the *Piano Concerto No. 2* by Prokofieff and the *Piano Concerto in G* by Ravel. As the course proceeds opportunities will occur for the presentation of concertos by Brahms, Schumann, Beethoven, Mozart, and Haydn. With proper motivation most of the students will begin to develop a curiosity to investigate the past. In one class, a boy was surprised to discover that George Gershwin did not invent the piano concerto! That Brahms and Liszt, before him, had already been rhapsodizing in music! A knowledge of blueprints, definitions, symbols, forms helped lead students to what was in the music. Plunging head first into classical waters is very much like being shot by a rocket into rarified air. The change in environment is not difficult to overcome, but with some groups it might be best to start with the atmosphere in which they feel more comfortable.

Who Should Elect the Course

The music literature course should be required for all music major students. There is nothing more barren than a technically trained musician who is unfamiliar with the materials of his trade. Professional instrumentalists tend to have little knowledge of the vocal forms and vocalists tend to know little about instrumental forms. The primary aim of teachers should be the training of well-rounded musicians. The broader the background, the better is the musicianship.

The course should be open to other pupils who wish to elect it. Amateurs and non-performers have much to gain from a course in music literature. The depth and thoroughness with which compositions are studied should lead to a wider and broader background on which to base a listener's growth. When the emphasis is on hearing a large variety of music, the familiarity with the content of many works tends to build a background for appreciation. In a five-period-per-week subject the content of the music literature course can be useful in preparing students for a lifetime of listening.

The Psychological Approach

In conclusion, we can learn from the examples cited here that the traditional, logical or chronological approach to the teaching of music literature is not always the best. A highly skilled teacher can use almost any approach and get results. There is an advantage to the psychological approach, however, in that it grows out of the needs and interests of the pupils. This does not mean that the class will concentrate ad infinitum on jazz and its influences on our serious forms. It does mean that if a student asks to hear *Finlandia* by Sibelius, this can lead to the hearing of *The Moldau* by Smetana, *The Roumanian Rhapsodies* of George Enesco, the *Dances from Galanta* by Kodaly, the *Suite of Ancient Polish Airs and Dances* by Panufnik, the *Rhapsody in Blue* by Gershwin and the *Grand Canyon Suite* of Ferde Grofé. A study of this wide assortment of nationalist and post-nationalist music literature can lead to the symphonies, concertos, and sonatas of the Romantic period when nationalism was so much in evidence. The symphonies, concertos, and operas can be explored with the use of scores, slides, and pictures, but at all times with an emphasis on the music. Great music has a way of selling itself. It is one of the functions of the teacher to tie together all of the individual contributions of a great composer so that a continuity for learning is created.

The appreciations teacher must guarantee the following practices in setting up a program for listening groups:

(1) The group must be exposed to a large variety of music—good examples of all styles, periods, and forms.
(2) Students must be free to explore for new knowledge from sources of materials which the teacher may suggest—books, recordings, newspaper and magazine articles, program notes of concerts attended.
(3) Pupils should be encouraged to build their own record collections in a purposeful and meaningful way.
(4) The group should be taken on field trips to hear concerts by local and visiting symphony orchestras, opera companies, and recitalists.
(5) Every effort should be made to present programs of good music in the assemblies. Here, teachers have a wonderful opportunity to reach all of the students in the school. Guest musical groups and soloists, in addition to talented school musicians, can make a positive contribution to the music education of the entire student body.

Materials and Equipment

The training of active listeners should also include making available for students, facilities and materials which are conducive for good listening. The music room should be equipped with fine record players and tape recorders which reproduce the beautiful sounds imprinted on recordings. Today, we have excellent stereo machines which are capable of replaying music recorded by the world's greatest artists. Students, in their homes and public places, have already been conditioned to and are familiar with beautifully recorded sound. In the school appreciation classes they should hear music played in the best possible setting. Good equipment is important for good listening.

Other Listening Opportunities

Listening opportunities should not be limited to the classroom. Provision should be made for one or more recording machines, with earphones, to be placed in the school library and in practice rooms, so that before school, after school, or during a lunch or free period, pupils can come to hear music. A library of records should be available so that students can make a free choice of listening materials. This allows for a rehearing of materials heard in class and in addition listening to recordings of their own choosing. Often, students will explore new areas of learning when not pressed to do so. They should be encouraged to use these facilities and materials.

Developing a Lending Record Library

Just as the library has books which pupils can borrow, there should be a lending library of records available for student use. These could be borrowed over weekends, or for longer periods of time, depending upon the size of and demand for the collection. Experience has proved that pupils take good care of the recordings, and the usual regulations which govern the loss or destruction of a book in the library can apply to recordings. Borrowed records can introduce listeners to the building of their own collections; they can help students to develop discriminating tastes. Every device should be used by teachers to encourage young people in our high schools to listen more actively to music.

A teacher of music appreciation and music literature was once asked: "How do you know whether your teaching of these subjects is successful?"

The answer was: "The most exciting proof of success that I have is that I see my former pupils at professional symphonic, operatic and recital performances that I attend."

Seven

Placing Music
in the
Overall Curriculum

The trend towards a broad program in general education is a good one. While specialization on the high school level is important, too often our schools tend to provide individuals with a narrow background for living and participating in today's world. The advances in the sciences and communications and new developments in the interrelationships of people throughout the world will demand a growing skill for coping with the problems of the individual and of the community. Music, when used in general education, can help students to see the interdependency of subject matter which until recently has been pigeon-holed and isolated in the curriculum. Using music in a program of general education can make the entire educational process more meaningful.

Using Music for Motivation

The use of music, and in fact all of the arts, in this manner, appears to be obvious. It is surprising, however, that the arts are used so little in connection with teaching other subjects in the curriculum. It may very well be that a shortage of teacher time is at the root of the difficulty. It is also possible that most teachers have not been indoctrinated along these lines. It is conceivable that our entire school program will have to be re-examined. Teachers of science, mathematics, social studies, English and foreign languages welcome any approach which will help interest and motivate pupils to greater effort. Music teachers, therefore, must be in the forefront in helping to plan a schedule which will permit the introduction of music into the general program. This is an approach to the organic curriculum.

Music and the Organic Curriculum

In the organic curriculum education is offered in a series of learning packages organized around a central core of subject matter. The learning packet consists of instruction programmed on a teaching machine, recordings, tapes, films, reading assignments, tests, and measurements. If we were to take *Fire* as a central topic, for example, one could study its physical and chemical makeup, examine it as a phenomena in nature and in man-made heat, learn to measure it, and study the way in which it affects animal and plant life. Students can learn about its use in war and in peace, how whole cities have been ravaged by it, how modern medicine uses it, and how man has learned to harness it. Authors have used the subject of fire in very dramatic ways, both in prose and in poetry. Artists have painted pictures which deal with the various aspects of fire. Richard Wagner has written, for example, the "Magic Fire Music" and the immolation scene from *The Ring of the Nibelungen* in which he fantasizes about the subject. There are many songs and instrumental compositions which are relevant to the study of fire. We can list a few:

> *Fireworks* by Igor Stravinsky (Descriptive music.)
> *Royal Fireworks Music* by George Frederick Handel (Highly idealized music written for a celebration.)
> *Forest of the Amazon* by Heitor Villa-Lobos (Contains a musical description of a forest fire.)
> *Il Trovatore* by Giuseppe Verdi (Includes musical descriptions of the anvil fires and a burning at the stake.)
> *The Requiem Mass in C Minor* by Luigi Cherubini (In the "Dies Irae" there is a vivid description of Judgment Day when sinners will burn in the fires of Hell.)
> *Gayne* by Aram Khachaturian (In this ballet the villain sets fire to the collective farm.)
> *The Trojans* by Hector Berlioz (Has several references to fire including the funeral pyre which Dido builds when she is betrayed by Aeneas.)

The educational packages are developed and prepared by teachers who are released from the classroom. Subject matter envelopes are designed for students to work on alone or in groups and each individual can move along at his own rate of speed. Some pupils may complete high school in less than three years; others may take more time than is usually required. Each package lists its own objectives and subject matter to be

Merin Studios, Philadelphia, Pa.

Figure 7–1: Music literature class discussing "Brunhilde's Immolation," from Gotterdammerung by Richard Wagner

mastered. Students test themselves when the body of work is completed, or can choose to be tested by the teacher who is available for consultation when needed.

The organic curriculum is broad in its concept. Resource people from universities, government, industry, the arts, and the professions should be available to make specific areas in the curriculum more meaningful. Minimum objectives should be set forth for the achievement of all students. The program requires guidance, supervision, and evaluation all along the way. The approach to the organic curriculum is one of developing a more creative atmosphere for learning.

How successful this type of curriculum can be is open for discussion, but this much is not open to question: we can learn much from its basic aims and objectives. Subject matter in the various fields of study is related and can be treated in that manner to the advantage of the learner. Music has already been proved to be an aid in the teaching of other subjects. Proper technics and materials will make the instruction more useful.

Utilizing the Music Teacher as a Resource Person

The alliance between the music teacher and teachers of other subjects presents an exciting challenge. Music teachers, as a part of their training, should have a knowledge of foreign languages, acoustics, literature, the social studies, and the other arts. They should be able to serve as resource persons in broadening the general education of pupils. From time to time it is desirable to bring music lessons into other classrooms. In almost every subject area music can help to motivate pupils to greater interest and participation. The connection results in greater interest in music also.

Scheduling Resource Teachers

Scheduling music teachers to go into a science or social studies class can create a problem, for music teachers, in the most flexible program, are busy and have little extra time unless scheduled in advance. There is no reason why the science and music teachers cannot exchange classes when they deem it advisable. The science teacher could teach music students a lesson related to the physics of sound, while the music teacher takes the science class for a lesson in how a clarinet is constructed and played so that it produces the quality which is associated with that instrument. Music and social studies teachers could be exchanged or combined in order to give both classes a better background for, let us say, the Civil War. A forward-looking administration in a school can actually set up several groups which meet together all year in order to utilize music, art and physical education instructors in an interrelated program. A European History course can be integrated with songs, symphonic and operatic music, some work in the history of art, lessons in languages, and a study of the folk dances of the nations involved. The mechanics for such a program can be worked out more easily at the beginning of the year when schedules are being set up. At meetings in which all of the teachers involved present tentative schedules most of the problems can be ironed out. When details are worked out long in advance no teacher will be unduly overworked.

Integrating Music and Science Teaching

Instructors, then, can establish technics for developing units in which subject matter is integrated. Music and science teachers, for example, can work out a course of study which leads to an understanding of the dual basis for music—that of sound as a science and sound as an art. While the artistic approach to understanding music is well established, there is a tendency to ignore the scientific approach. All avenues for developing understanding are important precisely because they help us to learn the true nature of the musical art. With modern developments in stereo sound, and acoustics generally, both music and science students can benefit from a mutual interchange of subject matter. This leads to learning in greater depth. The science student can learn from the disciplines taught by the music teacher. He can learn to listen more effectively to the sounds which heretofore and for the most part he only learned to read and see. The student of music through a knowledge of science can develop a broader concept of the tones which he produces and the music which he makes.

A violin student, for example, develops a better understanding of pitch and intonation when he discovers the ratio of two-to-one for the octave. The ratio for the pitches of the major triad is 3: 4: 5, making $\frac{5}{3}$ the fraction for finding the number of vibrations per second for the fifth degree of the scale, and $\frac{4}{3}$ the fraction for finding the number of vibrations per second for the third degree of the scale. True, in developing musicianship, the ear must be actively involved in the whole process, but scientifically, the entire scale can be worked out. The student of science and the student of music should both be aware of all available data. The production of musical tones on a brass instrument, with a knowledge of how the valves work, how added tubing lowers the pitches, how overtones are produced which involve the correct use of the embouchure, how the quality of the tone is affected by the shape of the bore, is subject matter which broadens the background of the student for more artistic accomplishment.

Finding the number of vibrations per second for each note of the scale reinforces the learning of arithmetical processes. A review of fractions and ratios can help the students to see the connection between the musical aspects of the problems and the mathematics involved. It is a matter of significance that pupils become involved in processes which are always available avenues for finding and using knowledge as they need it for the study of music or other subjects.

Studying Music as a Science

A knowledge of acoustics is beneficial to both the science and the music student. Scientists can help to answer the question, "What is music?" It suffices to say, here, that both the science and the music student must grapple with the problems of consonance and dissonance, and with the scientific aspects of pitch, tone, melody, harmony, rhythm, form, tone color, nuance, tempo, and dynamics. As one scientifically dissects music and then puts it together musically and artistically, one can come to a better understanding of what music is. All of the modern experimentation with sound can become more meaningful for students who are then in a position to evaluate the various theses propounded by scientists and musicians.

Studying Music as an Art

The large body of knowledge, both in science and in music, can lead to subject matter dealing with music as an art. How can a well-trained musician or acoustician understand the art of music without a knowledge of the scientific aspects of producing and reproducing music? Certainly, musicians from the very beginning have made music without an understanding of scientific phenomena. Everyone will agree, however, that the tuning of a violin is better accomplished if the player has learned not only to hear, but also to understand the significance of the perfect octave, the perfect fourth, and the perfect fifth. Scientific knowledge acquired by the musician helps to make him a better artist. The scientist, also, must benefit from a more complete grasp of the music. How else can he hope to make his discoveries more meaningful? Why is he studying this phenomenon in the first place? Periodically integrating music and science in a program of general education, therefore, has the decided advantage of making the learning of both subject matter fields more relevant.

Relating Music and History

The history of music parallels the history of civilization. Often, as one teaches the development of music through the ages, he tends to think of it as one large library of inventions in sound, totally unrelated to people and events. The sooner we depart from this approach, the better. In our attempts to get across the meaning of abstract musical works we have come to overemphasize the form, the beauty of the sound, all of the internal and external characteristics of what the composer put down on paper, and we have failed to show how inextricably the sounds are tied up with people. In the social studies class we discover how forces, movements, and ideas shaped the history of the world. It is not difficult to integrate music, therefore, which only reflects the existence of the same forces, movements, and ideas. Sometimes the music which is in the avant-garde reflects the advance thinking of an era and is regarded as such. At other times, as in the case of Johann Sebastian Bach, the music becomes a culmination or a summarization of an era. Surely the music of any period is documentary proof that man made his own destiny and recorded for posterity how he felt about it.

One of the best ways of teaching social studies is to include the use of the music and art of the period. The teaching of American history in high school is enhanced by the involvement of the arts. The songs and dances that George and Martha Washington knew are available for use. The minuets and gavottes were interchangeably used in early American history with the reels and schottisches which were imported from England. Native composers, such as Francis Hopkinson and William Billings, all made music which can be used in the teaching of our early American heritage. With the establishment of the city of Washington as the Capitol of the United States and the development of a vigorous social life in the city, came the institution of music as a social art. The claviers, harpsichords, and pianos of both Mount Vernon and the White House were imported from Europe and testify to the importance of music in the social scene. As our history grew, so our native music grew with it. Folk songs and dances developed as people, through their leisure time pursuits, expressed their feelings about an emerging nation. When our country began to move westward, music followed it all the way to California. Every war is reflected in our music. One could write and rewrite the history of our country in song, giving it a new dimension for understanding.

Many American composers have written musical works to describe and comment on historical episodes and events. Certainly an opera, such as *The Crucible* by Robert Ward, based on the famous play by Arthur Miller, is a searing document dealing with the early American witch trials. *A Lincoln Portrait* by Aaron Copland is a sensitive and impressive commentary on another period in our history. The entire Civil War period is well documented with songs and instrumental pieces which grew out of that era. All of the more recent wars have left their imprint on the music of our times. A variety of music from the World War I period, such as the famous songs by George M. Cohan or "the Stars and Stripes Forever" by John Philip Sousa, is available for use in the social studies classes, as are the folk ballads of the Dust Bowl era and the music of the great depressions and World War II.

In teaching European history, there is an even wider choice of music to draw on. There are vast operatic, choral and symphonic and folk resources available. Below, we list a few masterworks which deal with historical subjects:

    Tosca—Puccini
    The Trojans—Berlioz
    Benvenuto Cellini—Berlioz
    I Puritani—Bellini
    Norma—Bellini
    Don Carlos—Verdi
    Aïda—Verdi
    Il Trovatore—Verdi
    The Masked Ball—Verdi
    Nabucco—Verdi
    Hymn of the Nations—Verdi
    Boris Godounow—Moussorgsky
    Khovantschina—Moussorgsky
    Fidelio—Beethoven
    Incidental Music to *Egmont*—Beethoven
    William Tell—Rossini
    Water Music—Handel
    Pomp and Circumstance No. 1 and No. 2—Elgar
    Academic Overture—Brahms
    Fountains of Rome—Respighi
    Pine of Rome—Respighi
    Feste Romane—Respighi
    Marche Slav—Tchaikovsky
    1812 Overture—Tchaikovsky
    Emperor Quartet—Haydn
    Hary Janos Suite—Kodaly
    Alexander Nevsky (Cantata)—Prokofieff
    Peter and the Wolf—Prokofieff
    Finlandia—Sibelius
    Andrea Chenier—Giordano
    Rienzi—Wagner
    Die Meistersinger—Wagner
    Symphony No. 3 (Ilya Mourometz)—Glière
    War Requiem—Britten
    Threnody for the Victims of Hiroshima—Penderecki

Viewing Music as a Social Art

Many choral selections written in the Baroque, Classical, Romantic and Modern periods can be used to illustrate changes in the structure of society as history evolved. Certainly, the Bach Cantata, *Christ Lay in the Bonds of Death,* is as great a social document as any painting of the crucifixion or even that part of the New Testament which it describes. Each section of the *Mass in B Minor* by Bach can be viewed as a piece of social art. The "Et Incarnatus Est," the "Crucifixus" followed by the thrilling "Et Resurrexit" can be duplicated only by the great painters of the Crucifixion and the Resurrection. While Bach writes in the style of the Baroque period, the emotional content and coloring which he gives to these dramatic scenes transcend all periods and ages. High school students must see slides or prints of these paintings and hear the music in order to catch the full meaning of the composer's intention.

The shifting of forms and styles also reflects the changes in thinking which were coming into the world. When Marguerite, in Gounod's *Faust,* ascends into heaven after a wide assortment of sufferings on earth, she is rewarded by being allowed to ascend to the accompaniment of glorious music. Surely, Gounod, who was a devoutly religious man, was reflecting the philosophy of the times—namely, that the more one suffers in this world the greater will be the reward in the next one. The religious sequences in the opera are most dramatic in the context of the musical play. At times, however, they border on the oratorio style and are in a class with such static compositions as *Samson and Delilah,* by Saint-Saëns. Here also the shifting style reflects new ideas which were becoming popular.

Evolving Forms and Styles Reflect a Changing Society

From the Classical period, where the great emphasis was on form, it is difficult to pin down specific works and attribute social significance to them. The very fact that Haydn and Mozart wrote elegant and formal music for wealthy patrons is in itself a social picture of the times. It is difficult, for example, to understand the cheerful music of the "Concerto in Eb for Two Pianos and Orchestra," written by an unhappy Mozart when in the employ of the tyrannical Archbishop of Salzburg. Again, this was the sign of the times. Mozart, like Haydn the master craftsman, wrote music to order for special occasions and not necessarily as a reflection of his own feelings. The sensitivity of the music, however, reveals no lack of emotion. With deliberate thoroughness his seriousness of purpose creeps through. High school pupils can understand this, also. Today they make reference to such people as "those who use their advanced skills to please the establishment."

There are other evidences of evolving forms and changing styles in music history. With the music of Beethoven we begin to hear the stirrings of the French Revolution which are evident everywhere in the social scene. One can literally "hear" the man shaking his fist at the world. From his oratorio *Christus am Oelberg*, written in 1803, to the *Missa Solemnis* written 20 years later, we see a change in style and an increase in the ferment and excitement. As in the symphonies, however, the spirit of the man persists. All of these feelings culminate in the final movement of the *Ninth Symphony*, one of the most difficult and unrelenting pieces written to be sung. Here he reaches new heights of grandeur and drama. When an English translation of the words is read, students have little trouble in identifying with this "Ode to Joy." There is no finer example than this of the liaison between music and the social studies and its importance in the curriculum.

As Beethoven brings us into the Romantic period, we find a strong emphasis on nationalism with its folk song motives. There is a demand for more active listening, a need for stirring up and calming down feelings, and a desire to read a program into the music. The need to romanticize and mysticize the past, the necessity to analyze, criticize and evaluate the music, the demand to bring virtuosity to new heights, the placing of greater emphasis on intimacy and feeling, all lead to the new order, away from strict form and regulation. In studying this period, then, there is an easier opportunity to identify with social forces. Composers such as Schubert, Schumann, Brahms, all freely expressed themselves in the art song. Many of these have social content. Folk song motives began to appear in the symphonies, concertos, and sonatas; the emotional stirrings of the Romantics in literature and art began to be felt also in the music. Composers such as Mendelssohn looked back to the past romantically, and revived the St. Matthew Passion of Johann Sebastian Bach; Schumann and Berlioz not only composed but also wrote about music; and Paganini, Liszt, and Chopin brought virtuosity to new heights. Change was in the air. With it came the overthrow of monarchies and the establishment of more democratic forms of government by the end of the century. Certainly the great surge of Wagner, Bruckner, and Mahler toward mysticism tied itself eventually to Schopenhauer and Nietzsche, and became further evidence of the liaison between music and history. How can the history of the second half of the nineteenth century be taught without the music which grew out of it? The most abstract symphonies of Schubert, Schumann, Mendelssohn, and Brahms; the piano music of Liszt, Chopin, and

Schumann; the music dramas of Weber and Wagner were all a part of that history and identified with all of the social movements. The music teacher who sees the connection teaches the music in connection with the social forces at work here.

Relating Music and Foreign Languages

Music can play an important part in the teaching of foreign languages. Singing simple folk songs in French or Italian can give a language a flavor which it does not have when the verse is read alone. Christmas Carols such as "O, Tannenbaum" or "Stille Nacht, Heilige, Nacht" can be sung in German, "O, Carissimi" can be sung in Italian, "Minuit Chretien" ("O, Holy Night") can be sung in French. The "Marseillaise" sung in its original language is a favorite among high school students. Within recent times, the singing of French, Italian and German popular songs has become the vogue in the United States. "La Vie en Rose" and "Autumn Leaves" are popular French favorites. "Volare" and "Parlami d'Amore" are sung by American popular singers in Italian. The music teacher can come into the foreign language classes and teach songs in their native tongues. Combining the two subjects is not only a natural process; it also helps to motivate students for more exciting learning. The conversational approach, it has been found, is the best way to begin teaching a language. There are many students, however, who in their inexperience approach a new language with hesitation. Singing helps the process along.

The beauty of a language, the sheer sound of it well spoken, or well sung, can be a motivating force. In one class, the music teacher brought to the students of French a recording of *The Martyrdom of St. Sebastian* by Claude Debussy. The teacher had been called in to discuss French Impressionism and the part which Debussy played in its development. Each member of the class followed the script in French as Charles Munch conducted the Boston Symphony in the playing of the music and Vera Zorina recited the words in the original language. When this was completed, members of the class took turns in reading the many verses. Reciting and translating the words took several days. When the end of the poem was reached, the class again heard the complete recording. It was interesting to watch the students quietly mouthing the words along with the recording. Of equal importance was the fact that the class had undergone an unusual musical experience, one which is rarely achieved even in the concert hall. There isn't any question but that the class had received a more functional approach to the language and the music.

Later in the year the music teacher tried another experiment with the same class. Piano scores for the opera *Faust* were brought into the French class. After a brief explanation of the story, the class began to study the garden scene which includes some of the most beautiful music in the score. There is Faust's lovely "Cavatina," the comedy scene between Martha and the Devil, and the very sensitive "Love Duet." The music teacher explained how to follow the various parts of the score in both French and English. When, occasionally, the intense interest of the group was interrupted by a student who got lost in the score, the teacher quietly announced the page number and all students were back on the right track. The character parts were then assigned to members of the class, after which the words were enacted in French with different casts reading the lead parts. In the end, the class listened again to some of the music. Now, students mouthed the words with the recording.

Relating Music and English Literature

Assisting in the teaching of English literature, music can bring to pupils great literary masterpieces and help them to understand the works better. The study of music motivated by great literary works also has a merit of its own. Each important period has inspired great musical master-pieces which are based on literary texts. The Bible has inspired many deeply religious works. The poetry of Milton has inspired the composers Arne and Purcell and a number of other composers along the way. Shake-speare served as an inspiration to Verdi, Tchaikovsky, Britten, Schubert, Mendelssohn, Dvorák, Berlioz, Prokofieff, Gounod, Elgar, Liszt, Rossini, Smetana and many others.

Understanding the Difference Between a Play and an Opera—Othello and Otello

One music teacher was invited into an English literature class to com-pare the *Othello* of Shakespeare with the *Otello* by Verdi. The class had already finished reading the play when the music was introduced. Ex-cerpts from the opera included the "Love Duet" which closes Act I, "Iago's Credo," and the "Si Per Ciel" scene, in which Iago stirs Otello into a rage against Desdemona, from Act II. The "Willow Song," the "Ave Maria," and the final scene were heard from the last act. The music teacher ex-plained that for dramatic purposes a composer may drop some of the words and let the music itself serve as accompaniment for the action on the stage. At other times, the librettist embellishes the score with added words for greater dramatic impact. Arias or duets may be used to provide the contrast of delicate passages between two highly dramatic scenes. Verdi was a man of the theatre. He could not possibly have used all of the Shakespearian characters and their words. The music would tend to comment on all of the lines and cause endless delays in the action. Thus, in the Shakespeare play, if we are to take the final Death Scene as an example, after Desdemona is suffocated there is a long dialogue involving Emelia, Othello, Montano, Grattiano, Iago, Lodovico, and Cassio. Close to the end of the scene, when Othello can no longer find his position in life tenable, he stabs himself and recites two lines before he dies:

> OTHELLO: I kissed thee ere I killed thee; no way but this. (Falling on Desdemona) Killing myself, to die upon a kiss. (Dies)

Giuseppe Verdi, with the help of his librettist Boito, chose to let the music tell most of the story. He combined brief lines from several speeches which occurred earlier in the scene by Shakespeare. He eliminated most of the characters present so that Otello is alone with the body of Desdemona when he kills himself. This permits a dramatic aria which centers around the words: "Un bacio, un altro bacio" ("A kiss, another kiss"). Verdi chooses to have the orchestra comment on the tragedy while Otello expires over the body of his beloved.

The class, in the discussion which followed, seemed to have developed a keen interest in the workings of the theatre and the staging of an opera. Questions and answers which developed all led to "where can we see a performance of the opera?" Since performances of this music are rare, it is suggested that a complete performance of the work can be heard on long-playing records and tapes. Students can hear these performances and follow along with the libretto. The teacher also suggested reference materials, including the program notes prepared for the record album. A follow-up by the students, it was suggested, would help to build a better background for understanding and appreciation.

Comparing both of these masterpieces can lead to other great literary works which served as an inspiration for great musical compositions. There are a number of plays, novels, and poems that served as a basis for musical creation. Here, we list a few:

Literary Work	Author	Composer
Peer Gynt	Ibsen	Grieg
Midsummer Night's Dream	Shakespeare	Mendelssohn
		Britten
Prelude—Afternoon of a Faun	Mallarmé	Debussy
Pelleas and Melisande	Maeterlinck	Debussy
Ode to Joy (Ninth Symphony)	Schiller	Beethoven
Egmont	Schiller	Beethoven
William Tell	Schiller	Rossini
Lieder (Art Songs)	Verlaine	Debussy

Literary Work (continued)	Author (continued)	Composer (continued)
	Heine	Schubert
	Goethe	Schubert
Faust	Goethe	Gounod
		Berlioz
		Tchaikovsky
		Liszt
La Vie de Bohème (La Bohème)	Murger	Puccini
La Tosca	Sardou	Puccini
Eugen Onegin	Pushkin	Tchaikovsky
Poems (War Requiem)	Wilfred Owen	Britten
L'Allegro and Il Penseroso	Milton	Handel
The Marriage of Figaro	Beaumarchais	Mozart
		Rossini
The Bells	Poe	Rachmaninoff
Salome	The Bible	
	Oscar Wilde	Richard Strauss
Hamlet	Shakespeare	Thomas
		Tchaikovsky

Relating Music and Grammar

Theory and harmony are the grammar of music. It may be possible indirectly to assist the English teacher in the instruction of grammar. The creative process of composing a simple sentence, for example, is identical with that of composing a melody. A musical sentence can be broken down into the germ of a musical idea, a motive, a subject, a predicate, and modifiers. The presentation of a melody, as a musical sentence, can be handled as shown in Figure 7–2.

Here we find an elementary lesson in the teaching of sentence structure. Students who sing this, or a popular song with the same form, not only see but can also feel rhythmically how a sentence can be balanced. One lesson in which the music teacher brings in a variety of illustrations, first vocal, then instrumental, can clarify for the pupils the difference between a subject and a predicate, a thesis and an antithesis, a question and an answer, so that the whole concept of sentence construction is easier to comprehend. One can carry this further, of course, but how far the teacher takes this will depend upon the needs of the class and the ability of the instructor to carry it off.

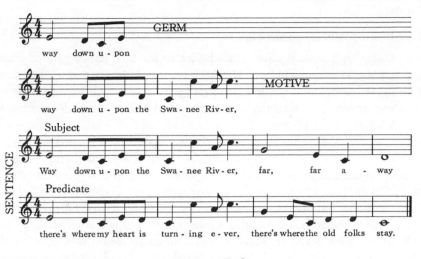

Figure 7–2

Teaching Music and Art

The art and music of any given period are strikingly similar. The integration of both subjects is important. Forms and styles have many similarities. How can anyone teach the music of Claude Debussy without showing and talking about the paintings of the French Impressionists? The emphasis on light, fleeting impressions and the use of new tone colors can be contrasted in art and music to develop a better appreciation of both subjects. There are startling similarities when one contrasts architecture with music. The Gothic arch, with its two curved lines meeting in the center at a given point, is similar to two phrases which are written to balance each other. Pictures brought into the classroom can show the relationships better. An impressionist picture of a boat gliding on the water can become more meaningful when the recorded piece "En Bateau" ("The Boat") by Debussy is played in class. Scenes from the French Revolution as painted by Delacroix take on new color and meaning when accompanied by the "Marseillaise" or the tribunal scene from *Andrea Chenier* by Giordano. The "Gleaners" by Millet grew out of the same school which created the "Angelus" of Massenet. "Pictures at an Exhibition" by Moussorgsky describes a visit to an art gallery where the paintings of his late friend Richard Hartmann are being shown. There are many illustrations of paintings in music. Bringing music into the art appreciation class helps with developing a greater appreciation for art and music.

Combining Music and the Dance

Many high schools have a fine ballet or modern dance group, where music plays an important part. Here the teacher is in a wonderful position to suggest background music for any program which will feature dancing. The use of music or dancing can originate in either camp. For example, one teacher, while preparing a performance of the American folk opera *Down in the Valley* by Kurt Weill, called upon the Physical Education Department dance group to prepare the Barn Dance sequence. The resulting collaboration served both the opera workshop and the ballet group well. On another occasion, a dance group wanted to dramatize a biblical subject and called upon the music teacher for suggestions. This resulted in an exciting ballet based on the Bible story of Shadrack, Mishak, and Abednego, with music by MacGimsey. The composition was sung by the choir and danced by the ballet group. Much choral and instrumental music lends itself to dance interpretation. We have all seen abstract works, such as the "Serenade for Strings" by Tchaikovsky or a highly descriptive piece such as the Prelude to *The Afternoon of a Faun* by Debussy used as a background for the dance. Music teachers are in an advisory position where they can often recommend compositions which will make for general educational growth.

There are many popular and folk compositions which lend themselves to choreography. From time to time new pieces of music are introduced with great relevancy for high school students. *Slaughter on Tenth Avenue* by Richard Rodgers is one of these. Another is *The Warsaw Concerto* by Richard Addinsell. A sophisticated choral arrangement of the Beatles' song "Yesterday" could be used as a backdrop for a modern ballet. The recent popular song "Little Green Apples" has a nostalgia which can easily be related to the dance. The folk-ballad "Elinor Rigby," popularized by many rock singers, has already been used by professionals as a dance pantomime on television. High school students can identify with this material and there are opportunities here for experimentation. Again, there is much to be gained from the collaboration of music and dance instructors.

Motivating Interest Through an Organic Curriculum

The potential for integrating music into the general education curriculum is unlimited. We have only been able to make a few suggestions here. All of the teachers, those teaching music and their collaborators, must be flexible and aware of the gains implicit in this teamwork. If we believe in a broad program of general education, we must clearly define the place of music in it. A shortage of teacher time will limit the amount of coordination with other departments. It is not difficult to see that in the near future, as additional specialists are hired in the music department, part of the teachers' time will be devoted to other departments in the school to help motivate and stimulate pupils to develop their interests in greater depth. Administrators, if they would like to utilize instructors in this way, will have to release them from the formal classroom to work part time on an organic curriculum in the school.

Eight

Organizing Effective
Assembly Programs

The assembly usually reflects the tone of a school. Here the gathering of students can be utilized for the development of morale, the acquiring of social and aesthetic values, and the presentation of subject material which lends itself best to mass education. It is important for assembly planners to understand clearly the implications inherent in a well-organized schedule. While we encourage talent and want to show it off, our prime function is educational. Every activity in the public school, including the assembly, should have its roots in the program of general education. The extent to which the program is successful will be determined by a clear understanding of the function of the teacher with regard to the morale of the school as it is reflected in the assemblies.

Functions of Music in the Assembly

Implicit in the concept that all school activities should be educationally oriented is the fact that assemblies should be used for developing good taste, appreciations, talent, and motivations for learning. Does this mean, then, that music in the assembly cannot be enjoyed or used functionally? Programs need not be dull. They should be informative, enjoyable, and entertaining. If planned properly, the assemblies should be an outgrowth of what is happening in all parts of the school.

The prime purpose of student gatherings should be the building of school spirit which will lead to an awareness of the school as a center of learning. School loyalty and morale are built on more than pep rallies. Pride in the achievements of students and graduates, those who are presented in the assemblies, can build a respect for the school and its offerings.

A secondary function of the assembly is to bring to the students programs and subject matter not always available for small teaching units.

A third aim is to encourage pupils, through observation and participation, to accept programs which encourage the development of better taste and understanding.

A broad general fourth objective can be the proselytizing, encouraging, and recruiting of students for participation in the many offerings found in the music and other departments. The assembly can present a unified picture of the music curriculum with the General Music Course at its base and the wide variety of specialties which grow out of it.

A final aim of the assembly schedule is the development of a good audience psychology as a valid part of the general education program for high school students. Proper audience behavior, the development of intelligent listening, the showing of respect for their peers who are performing or their teachers who are making presentations, are exercises in building good audience habits.

The important function of the assembly, then, is to unify all of these aims into a psychology for belonging to something as big and as important as the school, the disseminator of knowledge. All assembly programs should reflect a philosophy of education which runs parallel to that of the structure of the entire school.

Organizing the Committee

The assembly committee should be composed of student council representatives and teachers from various departments, including at least one of the music teachers. One of the administrators may also serve in an advisory capacity. Students must come to feel that they are involved in the planning. Opportunities should be provided for pupils to submit suggestions for programs in the assembly. As much as possible the schedule should be concerned with student presentations, participation, and involvement. If the student committee members are indoctrinated with the concept of the assembly as another avenue for enhancing their educational experiences, it should not be too difficult to de-emphasize the entertainment aspects of assembly programs and to enlarge the scope and accent on education. Teachers who sit on the committee may also make suggestions which will involve the participation of talented students and groups. Where the make-up of the committee is truly representative, the final list of programs scheduled for presentation in the assembly can be as varied as the participating members who formulate it.

Allotting Time for Assemblies

In most schools, assemblies are scheduled at a regular time each week. They vary in length from 15 minutes to an hour depending upon the program. If an assembly is well planned a great deal of subject matter can be presented in 15 or 20 minutes. Poor planning results in the wasting of time. It is better to make a presentation short and to the point. Programs which start and end on time and which are well paced and relevant are the most effective. There are special festival programs in which a number of groups will participate, and it may be necessary to extend the time for these to an hour, at the maximum. In those situations in which there are elaborate presentations which may extend for two hours or more, it is wiser to plan an evening concert. Utilizing large blocks of time in the school assemblies results in cutting short other scheduled academic work. In all programs, therefore, planning is important.

The Assemblies and General Education

Assemblies should be viewed as an integral part of the general curriculum. As such, all departments may contribute to the general education of the pupils. Sponsors of the public speaking class, the student government, the arts, physical education activities, teachers and department heads of the various subject fields—all can contribute to an exciting assembly schedule. When the Social Studies department assumes responsibility for arranging an assembly for a patriotic occasion, some music can be used to enhance the presentation and make it more relevant. Teachers in the music department should be scheduled to assist. There is no program in which music cannot be used to brighten and elevate the presentation.

There are many occasions in which the music teachers can help. A program presented for Washington's Birthday by the Social Studies Department may very well include some of the music which George and Martha Washington knew. Songs by Francis Hopkinson and William

Billings can be performed by talented pupils and several dances of the period can be demonstrated by a dance group with appropriate musical accompaniment. The Science Department might be interested in presenting a special film which deals with the exciting subject of acoustics. A number of music students could be used to demonstrate the principle of tube lengths, the amplitude of the wave, the two-to-one ratio of the octave, or tone quality. If the Home Economics Department is presenting its annual Fashion Show, in which costumes made by the class are presented, the Music Department can supply talented pupils to play appropriate music as the models parade in and out. The swearing in of new school officers, or the induction of new members into the Honor Society, could include appropriate ceremonial music played by the band or by a student on the organ. The use of music in assemblies should be relevant and appropriate at all times.

Listening Versus Active Participation

There are occasions in which the Music Department takes over the entire assembly program. Not too long ago, there was an era when most assembly programs included audience participation. Somehow, within recent years, there has been a tendency to use the high school assembly as a total listening forum in which students passively take part in the program and have little opportunity to participate actively in the presentations. There are two reasons for this:

First, in our American culture there is an ever-widening spectator approach to all of our educational and recreational pursuits. What has happened to the mass calisthenics, the Field Day in which the whole school participated, the Community Sings in school and out? Surely, some of these activities were too mechanical and sometimes defeated the objectives set up for them. Today we have substituted spectator sports and in music we have the Lewissohn Stadium, the Hollywood Bowl, Robin Hood Dell and Ravinia Park. There is nothing wrong with spectator activities; they, too, have their place in our culture. The point to be made here is that there are still goals to be set and achieved for mass student participation in many educational and recreational activities.

Secondly, we have become too highly specialized and enjoy presenting the products of our specialization. Of course, there should be opportunities in the assemblies for our most talented students. With the expansion of the general education curriculum, however, it is desirable that a more active participation of the entire assembly be encouraged. This leads us directly to the Community Sing and other programs in which the entire assemblage is unified. Every effort should be made to create an atmosphere of belonging.

The Community Sing

In those schools where there has been no community singing included in the assemblies, a great deal of patience will be required to build the proper kind of pupil participation. It will necessitate serious planning. The choice of material is important. Adolescents and teen-agers who have little or no background for participating in a singing activity tend to be shy when first involved in group singing. They gain confidence when the assembly singing begins to "sound." Motivation comes with a good choice of songs and the encouragement to sing out. The "Old Black Joe" and "Swanee River" days are gone. Today we have many exciting show tunes, folk and rock songs, popular ballads made famous by singers currently in fashion, and traditional patriotic and ceremonial tunes which still have relevance.

Song Materials

Times and situations change. Some popular songs become standards and many show tunes become an important part of the folk culture repertoire. Some of these, though not new, are still popular and are sung with regularity. The popularization of this material goes on daily by means of radio, television, and the record player. As lists are made up for the Community Sing new show tunes can be included. Others can be dropped as they fall into disuse and are no longer familiar. We list here a few show tunes which can be used successfully in assembly singing:

"The Girl that I Married" from *Annie Get Your Gun*—Berlin

"Summertime"
"I Got Plenty of Nothin' " } from *Porgy and Bess*—Gershwin

"The Man I Love" from *Girl Crazy*—Gershwin

"Old Man River"
"Just My Bill" } from *Show Boat*—Kern
"Make Believe"

"Smoke Gets in Your Eyes" from *Roberta*—Kern

"Some Enchanted Evening"
"Younger than Springtime" } from *South Pacific*—Rodgers

"You'll Never Walk Alone"
"If I Loved You" } from *Carousel*—Rodgers

"Climb Every Mountain"
"Do Re Mi" } from *The Sound of Music*—Rodgers
"The Sound of Music"

"The Surrey with the Fringe on Top"
"People Will Say We're in Love" } from *Oklahoma*—Rodgers
"Oklahoma"

"My Heart Stood Still" from *A Connecticut Yankee*—Rodgers

"Stouthearted Men" from *New Moon*—Romberg

"Who Can I Turn To?" from *Stop the World; I Want to Get Off*—Newley

"What Kind of Fool Am I?" from *Smell of the Grease Paint*—Newley

"Somewhere"
"Tonight" } from *West Side Story*—Bernstein

"The Impossible Dream" from *The Man of La Mancha*—Lane

Some assemblies, especially those called for special occasions, will require the use of carefully selected folk, popular, or foreign songs. We list but a few here:

Swing Low, Sweet Chariot (Negro Spiritual)
Go Down Moses (Negro Spiritual)
Jacob's Ladder (Negro Spiritual)
Ain't Gonna Study War No More (Negro Spiritual)
Sometimes I Feel Like A Motherless Child (Negro Spiritual)
We Shall Not Be Moved (Negro Spiritual)
Trampin' (Negro Spiritual)
Joshua Fit the Battle of Jericho (Negro Spiritual)
Nobody Knows the Trouble I've Seen (Negro Spiritual)
He's Got the Whole World in His Hands (Negro Spiritual)
John Henry (Chain Gang Song)
Kumbaya (African—Angolese Folk Song)
We Shall Overcome (Negro Song)
Dona Nobis Pacem (English Round)
Drink to Me Only With Thine Eyes (Old English Song)
O, Soldier, Soldier (Old English Song)
Stodele Pumpa (Czechoslovakian Song)
O, How Lovely is the Evening (Czechoslovakian Round)
Danny Boy (Irish Folk Song)
Kevin Barry (Irish Folk Song)
Zum Galli Galli (Israeli Folk Song)
Havah Nageelah (Israeli Folk Song)
Dayenu (Israeli Folk Song)
The Marseillaise (French National Anthem)
La Vie En Rose (French Popular Song)
Autumn Leaves (French Popular Song)
Alouette (French Folk Song)
Mariannina (Italian Folk Song)

Funiculi, Funicula (Italian Folk Song)
Santa Lucia (Italian Folk Song)
Volare (Italian Popular Song)
All Through the Night (Welsh Folk Song)
Marching Through Pretoria (South African Folk Song)
Peat Bog Soldiers (German Folk Song)
Cielito Lindo (Mexican Folk Song)
Waltzing Matilda (Australian Folk Song)
John Peel (Scottish Folk Song)
Comin' Through the Rye (Scottish Folk Song)
Red River Valley (American Mohawk Valley Song)
Blue Tail Fly (American Minstrel Song)
When Johnny Comes Marching Home (American Folk Song)
I Wish I Was Single Again (American Folk Song)
Down in the Valley (American Folk Song)
Hallelujah I'm a Bum (American Hobo Song)
Go Get the Ax (American Nonsense Song)
Casey Jones (American Railroad Song)
She'll Be Comin' Round the Mountain (American Railroad Song)
Yesterday (Popular Beatles' Song)

Technics for Improving the Tone

Many of these songs lend themselves to singing in barbershop harmony. This type of singing should be encouraged, as the fun aspects of it can lead to genuine interest in part singing. Faulty harmony can be quickly corrected in the assembly to make for greater enjoyment. Simple devices for better singing, such as producing the tone on a clear vowel, or dropping the jaw to get a more open sound will tend to improve the quality of the mass singing and render it more musical. Every effort should be made to encourage enthusiastic participation.

Patriotic and religious songs which can be used for holiday assemblies are suggested by the following list:

The Battle Hymn of the Republic
God of Our Fathers
Hail to the Chief
Columbia, the Gem of the Ocean
Yankee Doodle
America the Beautiful
When Wilt Thou Save the People
Come, Ye Thankful People, Come
Prayer of Thanksgiving (Dutch)
The Lord's Prayer (Malotte)
America the Beautiful

America
Star Spangled Banner
You're a Grand Old Flag
Yankee Doodle Dandy (Cohan)
God Bless America (Berlin)
. This is My Country (Jacobs)
Taps
Service Songs—Anchors Aweigh
        Marine Hymn
        Caisson Song
        Army Air Corps Song

Using Religious Music

Within recent years there has been much discussion about the use of special religious music and particularly the inclusion of Christmas carols in class and assembly programs. The decisions of the Supreme Court in 1962 and 1963 which cover the reading of the Bible, Christmas activities, and the use of special prayers, have tended to intimidate administrators and teachers. In some places the use of Christmas carols has been banned altogether. Without going into all of the ramifications of the law, some of the confusion can be clarified. It is not the function of public schools to indulge in religious education and the law is very clear on this. Most of the Christmas carols fall into the category of folk songs and can be used as such with discretion. It stands to reason that songs of an interdenominational nature are most desirable and can be used when relevant. It is also commonly agreed that a public school, which is open to all races and creeds, should exercise great care in utilizing material which is appropriate for a group. Certainly a theme such as "Peace on Earth, Good Will Towards Men" will receive objections from no one. There are many seasonal songs which can be chosen and which are appropriate for all students to sing.

The decisions of the Supreme Court did not eliminate the study of religion or the Bible as literature. Certainly, no study of western or eastern civilizations and cultures can be approached without references to and a study of the religions which were involved. The great musical masterpieces which grew out of these social and religious periods are an integral part of the subject matter to be studied. One cannot teach in an organic curriculum the relationships between the humanities and the social studies without references to religion and without hearing the great religious works of master composers. Religious teaching can be safely left to the various religious denominations who do a better job at staging religious pageants and demonstrations of faith. The only position which the music teacher can take is to use religious music, including Christmas carols, for educational and cultural enrichment purposes. There is a fine line here. No one really knows where religion ends and culture begins. If, however, we teach the Bible as literature or the Christmas Oratorio of Bach as music literature, these aspects of world culture can be accepted by everyone.

What are the implications for classroom and assembly singing? Certainly the music teachers can choose music for assemblies which are meaningful to all children. There is a wide range of song materials from which to choose. Here we list only a few:

The Twelve Days of Christmas (English Carol)
I Heard the Bells on Christmas Day (American Carol)
O, Christmas Tree (German Carol)
The Holly and the Ivy (English Carol)
Deck the Halls (English Carol)
Jingle Bells (Seasonal Song)
White Christmas—Berlin
Go Tell It On the Mountain (Negro Spiritual)
Sweet Silver Bells (Round)
To Bethlehem (Puerto Rican Carol)
Fum, Fum, Fum (Spanish Carol)

Radio and TV Technics

We also have, today, the community sing technics which have been developed for television and from which we can learn. The "Sing Along With Mitch" series a few years ago, the campus "hootenanny" which presented folk songs, and folk singers who encourage audience participation have established patterns which may well be used in high school assembly programs. Why not use talented students from the voice classes or the Folk Music Club to sing the verse of a song while the audience joins in on the refrain? Words may also be flashed on a screen overhead to give the audience confidence. The use of familiar devices and technics, borrowed from radio and television, may be another way to popularize assembly singing again and to bring about greater audience participation.

Leading Community Singing

The leader of community singing must have many skills at his command. While he must have the musicianship to supply a clear beat and phrasing which a mass audience can follow, he must also develop the personality to encourage, cajole, involve, and enthuse students. He must have the command to start and stop groups at will in order to make the singing clearer and more meaningful. He must be able to divide the assembly quickly into sections for part singing, which is extemporized and blended whenever possible. There is little musical excitement which compares with improvised barbershop harmony. Cadences at the ends of phrases, at the end of a refrain, or even whole choruses can be improvised and an enthusiasm for part singing can be built. Many folk songs, spirituals, and popular songs lend themselves to this approach. The song leader who can capitalize on this can build a good community singing program.

Homeroom teachers, who sit with their classes in the assembly, often ask for more community singing when the activity is exciting and inspirational. In one high school assembly, called to commemorate the assassination of Martin Luther King, Jr., there were a number of speeches and the choir sang. The most moving part of the program, however, came at the close of the program when the entire group arose to sing "Swing Low, Sweet Chariot." The spontaneous harmony united the group in common identification. All of the students and teachers filed out of the auditorium visibly moved. The song leader can weave magic spells and create moods, inspire, and unite his group. We need to train song leaders to recapture this art.

Part Singing in the Assembly

In some schools part singing is organized in the music classrooms and put together in the assembly. At one time this was common practice. Each tenth grade chorus class learned a number of part songs and when the tenth grade assembled for its weekly meeting it was not difficult to combine all groups for mass part singing. In those schools where roll was taken before going to the assembly students were assigned to seats by voices. Parts could be isolated for drill purposes. Difficulties arose when the policy for seating was changed and the various classes were assigned to seats by homerooms instead of by voice parts. In some places, where voices were unevenly distributed by homeroom seating, the quality of the singing tended to deteriorate; in others, some part work could still be maintained. Where community singing still exists, however, unison participation is most frequently the practice.

Today, in some schools, the National Anthem is sung in four parts, despite the lack of seating by voices, and despite the singing of the melody by a number of the boys the overall effect is quite acceptable. The doubling of the melody in octaves makes for a kind of spontaneous richness. It can be more exciting than the organized and formal approach. In one high school all seniors are required to learn the "Star-Spangled Banner" and the Alma Mater in four-part harmony in order to prepare for the graduation exercises which come at the end of the year. Once the parts are learned, the seniors practice the four-part singing at the opening and closing of each assembly. Each pupil learns to sing his or her part independently. The same procedure can be used for the singing of other song material.

Preparing Other Types of Programs

There are other types of music programs which are worth noting. Certainly, in every assembly series at the beginning of the year, there should be a presentation of all school music department offerings so that motivated pupils can choose an elective or extracurricular activity. Brief demonstrations and presentations by students can inform potential candidates about the content of each course or the subject matter emphasis of each extracurricular activity. Students already trained in the music department can sing or play selections illustrating the kinds of music and training which soloists and groups receive. A student from the General Music Course can explain how a group explores a course of study based on the subject "Music in Daily Living." Members of the music appreciation and music literature classes may explain the content of these courses and can perhaps describe a visit to the Municipal Concert Hall where a symphonic concert was heard or an opera performance was witnessed.

Preparing the Musical Quiz

There are other audience participation assemblies that are worth considering. Recently, because of the popularity of television quiz shows, a number of high school assembly programs began to schedule a session called "The Musical Quiz." Here, a panel of six students, three on each opposing team, became "experts" in the field of musical knowledge. Chosen in advance from the student body, the two teams vied for prizes. A moderator asked the questions and there were scorekeepers.

Questions which deal with music information can range from knowledge of the finest in concert music to the most sophisticated materials in the field of popular music. Some sample questions might be:

(1) Name the *Kings* who are famous in music:
   The March King (John Philip Sousa)
   The Waltz King (Johann Strauss, the Younger)
   The King of Jazz (Paul Whiteman)
   The King of Swing (Benny Goodman)
   A well-known popular singer who adopted "King" as his middle name (Nat King Cole)
   A famous "king," associated with New Orleans Jazz, who was addressed by that nick-name (King Oliver)

(2) Five famous marches will be played on the piano. Name the composition and the composer.

The Triumphal March from *Aïda* (Verdi)

March of the Children from *The King and I* (Rodgers)

Pomp and Circumstance No. 1 (Elgar)

Wedding March from *Lohengrin* (Wagner)

Stars and Stripes Forever (Sousa)

(3) What do you know about science and music?

    (a) In a pipe organ the pipes differ in size from very large and wide to very short and narrow. Do the larger pipes produce a higher or lower pitch? (Lower)

    (b) In an army bugle there are no valves. Various bugle calls are produced by adjusting the lips to the flow of air through the instrument. In the trumpet there are a series of valves to produce additional pitches. How is this accomplished?

    (Each time a valve is lowered a piece of tubing is added creating a longer tube-length. The longer the pipes, the deeper the tone. If we use different combinations of these valves we get a variety of tube lengths. All of these can be arranged in sequence to make up the scales which we use in music.)

(4) What do you know about the appreciation of music?

What is a symphony?

What is an opera?

What is a sonata?

What is a cantata?

What is an oratorio?

What is a folk song?

What is an art song?

What is counterpoint?

(5) A number of musical instruments used in symphony orchestras have been given special names in the field of popular music. What is:

A licorice stick? (Clarinet)

A horn? (Trumpet)

The dog house? (String Bass)

The coffin? (String Bass)

These are types of questions which can be used at a musical quiz. Others, no doubt, can be formulated from the various courses taught in the music curriculum. An eleventh grade team can compete against a twelfth grade team. A girls' group can be pitted against a boys' group. Prizes can be offered to winning contestants. This type of assembly stimulates an interest in the subject of music. If the stage crew for assemblies is versatile it can rig up a series of lighting panels with numbers flashing to actually simulate a television set-up. This can help create a more exciting program. The musical quiz is one more way of presenting subject matter in the assembly so as to motivate interest.

Using Musical Films

Many films which are designed for television and the classroom can be utilized to good advantage in the assembly. Some professionally pro-duced films come into the school libraries after being shown for a number of years in commercial movie houses. These, unfortunately, are too long for showing in the average assembly. There may be occasions, however, when the biographies of great composers can be shown. In one school, which has a 45-minute lunch schedule, full-length movies are shown in the auditorium with 20-minute installments given at the end of each lunch period. The life of Chopin, Schumann, Richard Strauss, or Beethoven could be exhibited with the accompanying music in short segments each day until completed. A number of these films are now available for rental at a nominal fee.

There are many educational films, originally designed for television, which run from 15 to 50 minutes, which can be rented for classroom or assembly use. Nineteen of the Young Peoples Concert Series conducted by Leonard Bernstein are available. Some of these titles include:

Jazz in the Concert Hall
The Sound of an Orchestra
Humor in Music
What is a Concerto?
What is American Music?
A Toast to Vienna in Three-Quarter Time
West Berlin Concert—Part I, Part II
Moscow Concert—Part I, Part II
Venice Concert—Part I, Part II

Instruments of the orchestra are demonstrated in a short film in which Sir Malcolm Sargeant conducts Benjamin Britten's *Young Persons' Guide to the Orchestra.* Leonard Bernstein also conducts a film entitled *What Does Orchestration Mean?* A short film entitled *A Bridge in Music* has been made which features the violinist Yehudi Menuhin and an Eastern musician, Ayana Deva Angadi. Both musicians compare the various styles of music from India and Cambodia with music from Italy, France, and Germany.

Many films have been developed which deal with the instruments individually and collectively. These are often on film for only ten minutes and can serve as part of a larger program dealing with instruments. Some of these films are:

> *The harp*—Ossian Ellis traces the history of the harp from the Bible. Additional film—Mildred Dilling
> *The violin*—Jascha Heifetz, Yehudi Menuhin
> *The cello*—Emanuel Feuermann, Gregor Piatagorsky, Paul Tortelier
> *String quartet*—Coolidge String Quartet
> *The horn*—Ifor James demonstrates the history and complexities of the French Horn—Part I and Part II
> *The trombone*—Alfred Flaszinski traces the history and development of the instrument.
> *The clarinet*—Jack Brymer demonstrates the mechanics of the instrument.
> *The percussion*—(1) Technics of snare drumming
> (2) James Blades and Joan Goosens trace the history of percussion instruments.
> *Peter and the Wolf* by Benjamin Britten—Characters are represented by pictures and the sounds of various instruments.
> *Organ*—The history of organ building
> *Guitar*—Andres Segovia
> *Discovering the Music of Africa*—Robert Ayitel, master-drummer from Ghana, and several associates demonstrate African percussion instruments.

Coronet Films has a series of short films which deal with instruments of the orchestra, showing how each one is held and manipulated, played alone and combined with others. These are shown in the four best-known categories:

> The Strings
> The Woodwinds
> The Brasses
> The Percussions

There are other sound films which picture and reveal the tone quality of orchestral instruments. The Paris Conservatoire Orchestra focuses on instruments of the orchestra by performing in the following ten-minute films:

> Carnival Overture—Berlioz
> Hungarian Rhapsody No. 2—Liszt

Eastin Pictures has a 20-minute film which deals with the choirs of the orchestra: "Blowing, Scraping and Banging Groups." This movie is entitled *Instruments of the Orchestra,* and is devoted to the sound of each individual instrument. Another similar film is entitled, *Toot, Whistle, Plunk and Boom.*

Pablo Casals, virtuoso cellist and teacher, has prepared a series of 25 half-hour master classes which were filmed at the University of California at Berkeley. Here we see the great master bringing his talent to the teaching of young cellists. Jascha Heifetz, the great violin virtuoso, is seen and heard as he applies his talents to the teaching of young students in a series of eight master classes. Andres Segovia, the great virtuoso of the guitar, in a series of 14 master classes, displays his great artistry in working with students from many nations. All of these master classes run for approximately 27 minutes. Each one is long enough to make an excellent assembly program.

There are a number of individual films which deal with the subject of the pianist and piano literature. The following pianists have recorded short sound movies:

Jan Paderewski
Josef Hoffman
José Iturbi
Jacob Gimpel
Artur Rubinstein
Vladimir Horowitz
Alexander Brailowsky
Glenn Gould
Vronsky and Babin

Many excerpts from opera are featured on educational films. Some are featured as a part of mixed concert programs; others attempt to tell the story through the use of a narrator and well-known selections. Below, we list a few:

Carmen
Aïda
Cavalleria Rusticana
The Barber of Seville
Faust
The Marriage of Figaro

For use in an integrated program there are films such as:

Science and Music—This deals with the sounds of music, showing loudness as amplitude, pitch as frequency of vibration, and quality as the relation between the fundamental and the overtones.
The Sounds of Music. (10 minutes)
Correlating Music with Social Studies—brings insight into the human meaning of the Negro spiritual, its origins, development, and characteristics. (30 minutes)

Music in Foreign Languages:
Italian—"Largo al Factotum" from *The Barber of Seville* by Rossini. Sung by Igor Gorin. (8 minutes)
French—*Carmen* by Bizet. A condensation. (25 minutes)
German—Marian Anderson Recital. Includes "Ave Maria" by Schubert. (28 minutes)

Films can be used in the assembly program when scheduled for a specific purpose. Each individual film should be chosen for its relevancy and appropriateness. For the most part, programs in the assembly should be live and films should be used with discretion. In those large schools which build a film library, motion pictures are often available as a substitute for a speaker whose appearance is suddenly cancelled or for other programs which do not materialize as scheduled. There are many fine films which can be utilized in emergencies. Most film programs, however, should be scheduled as a part of the continuous, supplementary, educational program. Surely, if Jascha Heifetz is coming to the community to give a recital, it would be an appropriate gesture to feature one of his short films in the assembly.

Utilization of Student Talent

Every opportunity should be used to present student talent in the assembly. Scheduling a performance for gifted students motivates them to greater efforts and encourages others in the audience to attempt the making of music. The utilization of skilled students need not be rigid or formal. If the pupil receives an award from an agency outside the school, or some other type of recognition, adding a three-minute piano or clarinet solo to an assembly program enriches the activity and sets up new motivations. If an outstanding student is to appear on television, a preview of the experience might be in order so that all students can be motivated to "tune-in" on the program. Many times this means that there will be an addition of three or four minutes to the schedule, time which can be obtained by cutting down on the "talk" aspects of the program.

It is not always desirable to present whole programs of musical talent. There are times when it is better to inject one musical selection in an otherwise non-musical program. This can have a decided advantage; many assemblies which are made up of all talk features become more interesting when broken up with some music. If the music which is planned is appropriate, the mood and character of the presentation can be made more relevant. The use of some music in each assembly program also makes it possible to point up constantly the importance of music in daily living. The use of music in this way, no matter how brief the interlude, makes for greater student interest.

Using Alumni Talent

From time to time it is of great importance that alumni who are successful in the field of music be invited to appear before the school assembly. Where a music curriculum is successful graduates who return for visits to the school can add inspiration and motivation in the curriculum. Advance publicity through the daily school flyer, intercom system, and posters can publicize the event. The program can take on the form of a short recital. It may include a special alumni award and perhaps a brief inspirational talk to inspire others who are preparing for a career. All in all, a student who is sitting in an auditorium seat where a well-known, successful artist formerly sat, cannot help being proud of attending a school which has helped in the training of such an artist. All of these alumni soloists need not already be launched on a concert career. Sometimes a graduate who is studying at a college or conservatory can return to give a performance which shows progress. The music teacher should use every possible motivation in the assembly program.

Planning Concert and Festival Programs

Large assembly concert and festival programs, those which run for 45 minutes to an hour in length, can become annual events of great importance to the music program. They should be differentiated from full evening dress-up presentations which are planned for parents and the community. There is a place in the assembly schedule for the Annual National Music Week Concert, the Annual Spring Concert and the Annual Christmas Holiday Program in which all school music groups appear. In planning the program, emphasis should be placed on balance, enthusiastic participation, and audience involvement. While some of these programs may be more serious than others, those featured in the regular assembly schedule should utilize the "something for everybody" approach. This does not mean playing down to the audience. Implicit in this is the necessity for students in the audience to be able to identify with the performers and the music being performed. There are times when we tend to become too "high-brow" and scare off the customers.

Below is listed a Christmas holiday season program, performed in a large city high school, which was an hour in length and was presented on the day before the approaching holiday:

Program

Christmas Overture (Owens)	School Orchestra
I Wonder as I Wander (Niles)	
Carol of the Bells (Russian)	
Fum, Fum, Fum (Spanish)	Vocal Ensemble

Deck the Halls
White Christmas (Berlin) .... Community Singing
'Twas the Night Before Christmas .... Narrator
                                                     School Orchestra

Spring Carol from *A Ceremony of the Carols* (Britten)
What You Gonna Call Your Pretty Little Baby (Spiritual)
Noel, Noel (French) .... A Cappella Choir
And the Glory of the Lord $\Big\}$ from *Messiah* (Handel)   A Cappella Choir
Hallelujah Chorus   ....   Vocal Ensemble
                                                   Organist
                                                   School Orchestra

The annual spring concert allows for a greater variety of material. Here again, all school groups can be involved in the project. In one large city high school the following program was given:

Program

Overture to Mignon (Thomas) .... School Orchestra
Adoramus Te (Palestrina)
Blow Trumpets Blow (James)
Black is the Color of My True Love's Hair (American Folk)
What Shall We Do with a Drunken Sailor (Bartholomew)
                                                   .... Boys Glee Club
With Drooping Wings from *Dido and Aeneas* (Purcell)
I Have Twelve Oxen (Malin)
I Know Where I'm Goin' (Scott)
The Old Woman and the Pedlar (Davis)
                                                   .... Girls Glee Club
Selections from *La Pericole* (Offenbach) .... School Orchestra
God Be In My Head (Traditional Interdenominational Hymn)
Flo Me La (African Walking Song—arr. Simone)
Benedictus (Paladilhe)
Sweet Patatah (Southern Song—arr. Simeone) .... Soprano, Tenor Solos
                                                   .... A Cappella Choir
Joshua (Moussorgsky) .... Boys Glee Club
                                                    Girls Glee Club
                                                    A Cappella Choir
                                                    School Orchestra

In smaller schools, where the schedule of offerings is sometimes more limited, the assembly program which is presented may still have variety.

The content, of course, will vary with the abilities of the participating groups. The quality of the program, however, should be of a high order and reflect the versatility of the teachers involved and the variety of the offerings in the school. Each program should have material of a serious nature and contrasting music which is lighter. Large or small, the school assembly program should reflect the growing musicality of the students.

An interesting spring concert presented in a small high school assembly utilized the glee clubs and the school orchestra:

Program

Overture—Selections from *The King and I* by Rodgers

.... School Orchestra

Ave Maria (Arcadelt)
John Peel (Scottish)
Pilgrims' Chorus from *Tannhäuser* (Wagner)
There is Nothing Like a Dame from *South Pacific* (Rodgers)

.... Boys Glee Club

The Spirit Flower (Tipton)
All Glory, Laud, and Honor (Teschner)
At the Gate of Heaven (Mexican)
Ho-La-Li (Luvaas)

.... Girls Glee Club

Selections from *The Student Prince* (Romberg)

.... Boys Glee Club
Girls Glee Club
School Orchestra

Assembling students in the school auditorium requires an overall plan. The organized series of programs must grow out of the philosophy on which the whole program of general education rests. The main function of the assembly series is to develop school morale and social and aesthetic values, and to present those educational materials which lend themselves best to mass instruction. Every activity in the assembly should be related to objectives in the program of general education. While the programs should be interesting and motivating, the prime emphasis should not be on entertainment. Teachers can leave this to professional entertainers. The assemblies can serve a most important function in the well-planned educational schedule. They should unify all of the objectives so that students ultimately come to understand them as another place in the school where morale is built and knowledge is disseminated.

Nine

Performing in

Concerts, Festivals,

and Contests

Organizing for Mass Education and Mass Activity

If the organizing of the music curriculum with all of its varied and exciting extra-curricular ramifications is a complicated matter, preparing to show off the work of the many courses can only result in complex procedures. There is much more to giving a concert than preparing students to play and sing. One should see in these large activities the necessity for detailed organization. In music education there are many opportunities for exhibiting the work of individuals and combined groups. There should also be opportunities for any student to express himself by participating in large groups. Through mass activities many pupils can identify with others very much like themselves and with the ideas inherent in music which great masters have created. This, of course, is one of the strong objectives of music in the general education curriculum.

Benefiting from Mass Activity

Music teachers who conduct a wide assortment of activities must be organized if they are to see the results of this work shown off in a mass activity. In addition to the public relations aspects of performing in public, it is desirable for the students themselves to learn and benefit from taking part in mass performances. Here, we sometimes have hundreds of pupils involved in exercises of patience, cooperation, goodwill, charity, mature behavior, thinking, and leadership. The very act of participating tends to encourage each pupil to fall in line and work for a group result. Organizing for mass activities pays off.

Organizing Student Committees

A positive means of getting students to identify with the musical program is to involve them in committees which help the various organizations to move in the right direction. Committees of pupils can be arranged to assist with the many chores which must be handled in connection with routine preparations for any musical event. There are Publicity and Advertising Committees, Ticket Sales Committees, Robe and Uniform Committees, Stage and Set Committees, Music Librarians, Ways and Means Committees, and Social Committees. Each group has its own functions and contributes to the success of the venture. Many high school pupils are well able to assume responsibilities which lighten the burden of the teacher. Here it is important to involve as many choir, band, and orchestra members as possible. Students should develop a feeling of belonging. Where pupils are directly involved, greater interest results and the success of the musical program is inevitable. One of the outcomes of involvement should be the development of leadership qualities in as many pupils as possible.

Performing in School

The advantages of performing in the community must be weighed against performing in the school. It is usually desirable that performances should be given in the school and the public should be invited to attend. There are a number of advantages to this: (1) it makes the school the center of the music education program; (2) the emphasis is placed on the educational aspects of the activity; (3) the selection of the music is influenced by the function of the program; (4) the facilities for presenting a concert are usually better in the school than in a public hall or a recreation center; and (5) the mechanics for staging a program are simplified and minimized.

Performing in the Community

However, performing in the community may have desirable outcomes, such as: (1) the development of more diversified programs; (2) the development of an excitement and enthusiasm for music, in school and out; (3) encouraging students to work for greater musicality; (4) helping to raise standards of performance because of additional motivations; (5) exposing the community to different kinds of music; and (6) interesting the community in supporting a broad program in music education.

The number of programs scheduled in the community should be determined by the advantages to the students and to the school program. Preparation for large mass activities, away from home base, can be time consuming. There can be disadvantages to a large number of outside activities. There are some schools where the choir and band rarely perform for their fellow students in the auditorium but are regularly scheduled for performances outside of the school. Most of the high school pupils carry a full roster of academic subjects. It is not fair to burden them with activities which interfere with their preparation for another career. In one large city, a deservedly popular choir, by invitation, took part in 22 Sunday performances in one year. The schedule was eventually changed because parents felt that students should spend more time with their families over the weekend. The focal point of their activities has now become the high school auditorium.

The band, in presenting public concerts, has tremendous entertainment potential and as such will tend to be exploited. In many towns and cities, bands combined in a festival are called upon to perform at civic, patriotic, and community spectaculars. The music at these functions is chiefly chosen from military and college catalogues, radio, television, and the theatre. While most of these selections are desirable in themselves, all of the music used is chosen with an eye on the entertainment values of such a program. A greater effort should be made by band leaders to broaden the repertoire and scope of such programs. An attempt should be made to include some of the fine music written and transcribed for the concert band. The use of a transcribed prelude by Bach, or standard concert overtures, or symphonic suites, can give the band greater stature. At the same time the utilization of this music will present another avenue for the musical growth of the students involved. In the light of modern music education objectives, emphasis should be placed on the growth in musical education that comes in preparing for a performance. There is more to music education than entertainment.

Working for Broader Objectives

The same can be said for choral organizations which are called upon to perform at combined community festivals. The choirs which specialize in show tunes and sophisticated arrangements of popular songs exclusively are working toward limited objectives and look only to programs which will entertain. In many of these groups students learn music by imitation and rarely develop technics for reading or performing musically. Teachers and administrators who encourage this approach are not serving their true function which is to educate first and entertain second.

Relating Concerts to Musical Growth

There are, of course, a number of opportunities for the performance of out-of-school concerts which are directly related to the musical growth of high school pupils. The music director must be selective. From time to time, professional and semi-professional orchestras will invite high school choirs to sing a work of major importance. A number of years ago, Eugene Ormandy invited three high school choirs to sing in a performance of the Brahms' *Requiem* with the Philadelphia Orchestra. This was a musical experience which left a lasting impression on the students who participated. Several years ago the Germantown High School Concert Choir, in Philadelphia, was invited to participate in a concert by the Wissahickon Valley Symphony Orchestra, a community group composed of professionals, semi-professionals, and talented amateurs. It was decided that the program would include representative choral compositions of all faiths, nationalities, and races. The parents who attended and the students who participated in the program all benefited from the experience. The program for the concert is shown in Figure 9–1.

Motivation for Educational and Emotional Growth

There are few high school students who are mature enough to want to rehearse for the sheer joy of playing together. Motivation through planned concert programs, therefore, should be thought of as opportunities for educational and emotional growth. The training which goes into a rehearsal for a concert, the choosing of the music, the development of musicality, the development of rapport all work towards the presentation of a better performance. Performing, then, is the end product of what is taught in the classroom. True, the teacher chooses music with an eye on the spring concert, but if he is working towards the attainment of general educational objectives, the emphasis on musical growth can only result in a better spring concert.

All of these performers tend to become competent amateurs and a few will become professionals. Through motivations connected with rehearsals and performance, students become more conscious of the importance of musicianship. A concert of excellent quality can only result in the creating of musicians, amateur and professional, who are better in-

The WISSAHICKON VALLEY *Symphony Orchestra*

THIRD CONCERT
May 11, 1961, at Eight-thirty
Germantown Jewish Centre
Lincoln Drive and Ellet Street
Philadelphia

LOUIS VYNER, Conducting
DAVID MADISON, Concert Master
HARRY E. MOSES, Guest Conductor

GERMANTOWN HIGH SCHOOL CONCERT CHOIR

. . . Program . . .

Prelude to Act III — "Lohengrin"..Wagner

Symphony No. 8 — B minor "Unfinished"..Schubert
    Allegro moderato
    Andante con moto

INTERMISSION

Dies Irae from Requiem Mass in C minor..Cherubini

He Watching Over Israel from "Elijah"..Mendelssohn

Hospodi Pomeelui ....Lvovsky

Psalm 150 ....Lewandowski

Great Gitten Up Mornin'
        Harry E. Moses — Conducting

Battle Hymn of the Republic..arr. by Wilhousky

★ ★

This concert is made possible by a grant from the Trust Funds of the Recording Industries, in cooperation with Local #77, American Federation of Musicians of Philadelphia.

Figure 9–1

Figure 9–2: Performing out-of-school concerts in conjunction with community musical organizations can be related to the musical growth of

terpreters of music and more active listeners. Pupils, here, are exposed to a wide variety of music. All of it cannot be performed. Some of it may have been chosen to develop reading skills and rhythmic or vocal technics. Other music may have been chosen for appreciation purposes. The program which is finally chosen by the teacher and the group for performance is, then, selected from a large repertoire of representative works. Acceptance of a poor performance of such compositions may develop misconceptions of what this music can mean in the life of the producer. Inversely, an excellent performance has lasting outcomes which leave a permanent mark on the students involved. Every activity, including the concert performance, should be used to make students more musical.

Seating Large Numbers of Performers

The larger the number of students participating, the more careful the advance planning should be. Often, where space is limited, special platforms will have to be constructed on which the performers will sit. In some cases it may mean that individual performing groups will have to remain backstage until called upon the platform to perform. A special arrangement may be necessary for the final grouping to perform combined selections in which all of the pupils participate. Massing for large festival programs is a problem and each director must work out an arrangement in accordance with his own facilities. One seating chart for a spring festival looked like the one illustrated in Figure 9–3.

The Music Festival

Another setting for a mass participation festival involves the use of a large stage and a smaller platform in the orchestra pit for individual smaller group presentations, as shown in Figure 9–4. We differentiate here between regular assembly festival programs and large mass activities which are given in the evening for parents and the community. The kinds of festival and concert presentations which are developed for public reactions will depend to a great extent upon the educational philosophy of the administration and the music teachers. Where music is related to the needs of the entire general education curriculum, administrative support should be forthcoming. There are various types of programs which will meet these objectives:

(a) *The music festival in which all school groups participate.*

Here we find the combined presentation of the choir, vocal ensemble, glee clubs, solos, duets, trios, and quartets; the orchestra, band, smaller instrumental ensembles, and instrumental soloists. Featured in the pro-

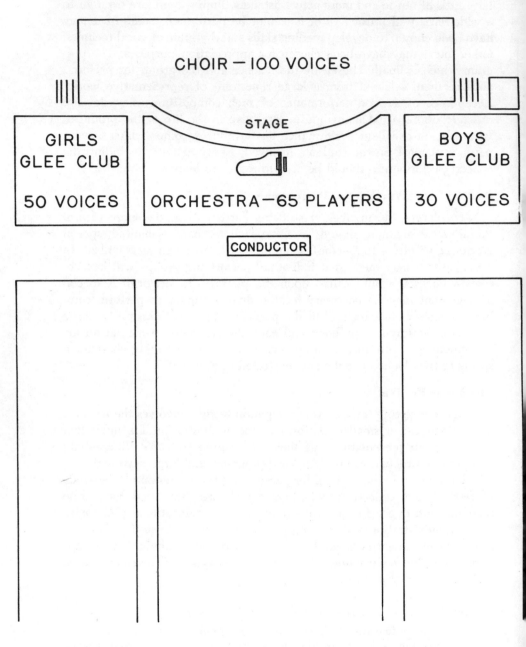

Figure 9–3

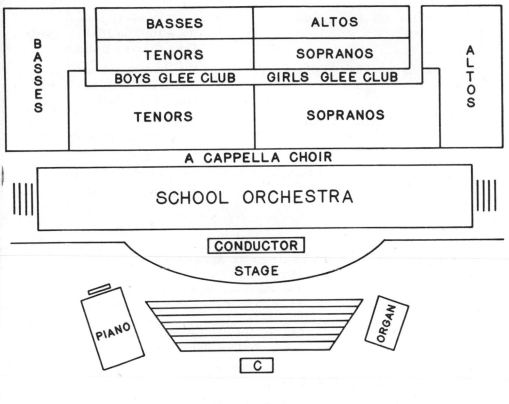

Figure 9–4

gram may be original compositions by students from the creative music classes. Student conductors may be prepared to lead some of the selections. Music appreciation and music literature pupils can prepare the program notes. The main purpose of such a program is to show the variety of activities which make up the music curriculum.

(b) *The opera workshop presentation in which the choir, vocal ensemble, and glee clubs participate.*

A school which has a variety of voice classes and perhaps an opera workshop could stage an all-operatic program. One high school program featured the following music:

Program

1. Don Giovanni (Mozart) .... La Ci Darem La Mano
(Give Me Your Hand, Beloved)
Duet—Soprano, Baritone

2. La Forza Del Destino (Verdi) .... Solenne in Quest' Ora
(Swear in This Solemn Hour)
Duet—Tenor, Baritone

3. La Traviata (Verdi) .... Parigi, O Cara
(Back to Paris, Beloved)
Duet—Soprano, Tenor

4. Porgy and Bess (Gershwin) .... Bess, You Is My Woman
Duet—Soprano, Baritone

Intermission

5. Down in the Valley—An American Folk Opera (Weill)
Student Soloists, Choir
Two-Piano Accompaniment
Violin Soloists for Obligatos and Barn Dance Sequences
Choreography by Physical Education Department.
Sets by Art Department.

Finale sung by Pit Chorus, composed by the combined Choir, Vocal Ensemble and Glee Clubs.

(c) The operetta and the musical comedy

Staging an operetta or a musical comedy takes a tremendous amount of preparation and effort. Some productions are quite elaborate and offer a pleasurable evening of entertainment. The project helps to develop talented individuals. Many famous stars in the theatre point with pride to their beginning experiences in high school. One cannot help but ponder, however, on the cost in time and effort. Many of these productions are rehearsed for months, before school, after school, in the evenings, on Saturdays, and on Sundays. Long hours of practice must deprive students of time which should be devoted to other activities. Most teachers and administrators weigh the advantages and disadvantages before deciding to mount a stage work.

Where performances can be given without sacrifice of quality education, they are more than justified.

The financial risks of staging a copyright-owned show must also be taken into consideration. The composer and the publisher are entitled to the royalties involved. Costumes and scenery for an elaborate production are expensive and subtract from the income which such a production might bring to the music department. The advertising and the ticket sales campaign take time and work. The educational increment from such an activity is necessarily small and the music educator must weigh its value against more profitable uses of the time. Music education has now come of age. It has been influenced greatly in the development of standards and sophistication by radio, television, and the theatre. The teacher who plans such an activity must ultimately decide how important it is to the school and the community.

Music teachers have helped to stage such shows as *Oklahoma, The Red Mill, My Fair Lady, Paint Your Wagon, Brigadoon,* and *Annie Get Your Gun.* Many of these are fine productions. It must be remembered that many small communities do not have visiting musical companies, and the high school is the only place where a performance can take place. The school production meets a definite need. Where such extravaganzas are mounted, however, care should be taken that the school work of the participants does not suffer, nor should this activity be used as a substitute for any of the other activities in the music curriculum.

(d) *The musical revue and variety show*

The musical revue and variety show still are the favorites in many high schools throughout the nation. The mounting of these shows is not usually the sole responsibility of the music department. The basic outline for a show of this type usually includes the various musical organizations, dance groups, the drama club, the gym team, a drill team, some comedians, and skits. It is the music, however, which ties the whole program together. Here, again, is another opportunity to show off most of the talent in the school. Soloists and individual groups can be rehearsed separately and the entire show can be put together in two long rehearsals. The most difficult part in putting on a show of this type is to know how to balance and cut it so that it does not lag. In order to keep the program moving, solos, duets, and short skits can be performed in front of the main curtain. This will permit sufficient time for the backstage crew to prepare for the next large scene. The mechanics for a smoothly moving show must be worked out and rehearsed in advance.

The music department has the responsibility for whatever appears musically on the program. There is room in the variety show for the finest in popular music. Young people today have sophisticated taste acquired through listening to recordings, the radio, television, and the movies. The high school stage band must aim for a high standard of musicianship and performance. It is the school instrumental and vocal teachers who help set and maintain the goals. Whether popular or concert music is performed, the pupils will label it "corny" if it doesn't meet a comparative standard of sophistication.

The background for the dance and ballet sequences, the gym teams, and the skits must be supplied by the music department, when music is needed. Students who play the piano or organ or who play in small combinations of instruments can be taught to accompany and thereby supply the continuity for the program. This is invaluable training for the instrumentalists and the added participation is more entertaining for the audience. In one variety show, a choral group sang the popular song "Tuxedo Junction" as the background for a modern dance episode. In another review the band played "Slaughter on Tenth Avenue" by Richard Rodgers as a background for a dance pantomime. Combining groups in this way makes for an exciting joint effort, and the results are usually rewarding. Again, if we aim to achieve a high standard, the overall program can be successful.

(e) *Cantata and oratorio performances*

The performance of great choral masterpieces is a fine avenue for the development of musical growth. Through these special concerts large masses of students can be involved. One technic for utilizing groups, in addition to the choir, is to have the vocal ensembles and the glee clubs join in singing the larger and broader choruses of a masterwork. The *Christmas Oratorio* of Camille Saint-Saëns lends itself to such treatment. The main body of the work is sung by the choir and selected soloists. Additional choral groups can join in the singing of the final chorale which is not difficult musically. The massive sound at the end of the performance gives the music added majesty.

Exposure of the choral groups, and eventually the audience, to great choral masterpieces such as these is most important. Music lovers rarely get to hear these works in performance. A number of churches still perform great choral masterpieces from time to time, but unfortunately, most high school students will never get to hear this music if the music department of the school does not undertake the study of the selections. When we add the participation of a large number of students, the experience can become increasingly more meaningful.

Some choral works are too long and too difficult for high school groups to perform adequately. There is no reason why excerpts from a work cannot be given. The "Requiem Aeternam" from the *Manzoni Requiem* of Giuseppe Verdi is a beautiful selection which can be sung apart from the complete work. It is more desirable that the Christmas or Easter portion of the *Messiah* by George Frederick Handel be given in a good performance than to attempt the entire work, which is too difficult for a high school choir. Some schools perform three or four choral excerpts from the work with selected solos interspersed to create an inspirational mood. Again, a smaller choral group can sing most of this program, with the combined choruses and orchestra presenting a stirring finale with the "Hallelujah Chorus." Emotionally moving climaxes and program endings prepare an audience for the realization of the wonderful power of music. That, after all, is one of our most important aims—to utilize the power of music for the cultural development of our students.

Musical Contests

All educators agree that attendance and participation of groups in a festival is a wonderful experience. There is much evidence now, however, to document a national opposition to musical contests as such. In its place, music educators almost everywhere are substituting the non-competitive festival, the city-wide, state-wide, and regional concerts. Many teachers are reluctant to enter groups for either competition or adjudication. Some schools have better facilities and more opportunities to practice. In one town a choir may be scheduled to meet three times weekly, in another five times weekly. Some schools have smaller budgets for music and instruments; others have colossal appropriations. Is it not unfair to pit these groups against each other in competition? In a real sense, underprivileged groups start out at a psychological loss. Would it not be better, then, for all groups to appear: (1) to learn from each other; (2) to be evaluated by a group of adjudicators who have before them a filled-in questionnaire which describes the nature of the performing groups; (3) to come out of the activity motivated and inspired to practice for improved skills and results? It is not the function of educators to show off. Everything that we do in music education should add up to an opportunity for musical growth.

Performing in concerts, festivals, school shows, and contests will require much organization. Music teachers must measure their plans against the philosophy which underpins the entire music curriculum. Almost every conceivable mass activity is possible for performance. The factor which will decide whether or not to undertake an activity will be its potential for musical growth. Enjoying and being entertained by a musical performance are important. Developing a festival, show, or concert just to amuse and entertain, however, has little educational value. Utilizing these activities as a spawning ground for a fruitful program of music education is more valuable.

Ten

Scheduling and
Giving Credit for
Music Subjects

Basic Purposes of a Music Schedule

The basic aims of a well-planned high school schedule are: (1) to allow students a wider selection of electives; (2) to encourage larger numbers of pupils to choose a variety of academic and non-academic subjects; (3) to allow for a rotating system of selection which will broaden the general education of the students and (4) to arrange more preparation and planning time for teachers. These objectives should be taken into consideration in the planning of the music schedule. If the music program is broadened to function as a part of the curriculum in general education, much music can be integrated with other subject matter. Where highly developed skill courses are included, the number of students enrolled will of necessity become more limited. For those pupils who tend to work toward a professional career, however, all courses will offer an educational background on which to base a specialization.

Scheduling Based on Need

How can music classes be scheduled most effectively as a part of a curriculum in general education? A large variety of schedules have evolved, revealing differences in philosophy that have grown up around the problem. Where educators feel that music is important to an educational program, it not only survives but it also grows in scope. Where educators create a curriculum top-heavy with the specialties, the program meets the needs of only a small percentage of the students. Music classes, then, are fewer in number and for the most part extracurricular. The schedule, like every course within it, must be designed to meet specific needs within a school. Large high schools, of necessity, will require a different kind of program from that found in smaller schools. The number of teachers available for the scheduling of activities is a factor. The special skills of each teacher must be given consideration. Flexibility in scheduling, then, should lead to a large variety of activities which are based on need.

Scheduling Based on Teacher Flexibility

Implicit in the concept of a flexible program is the choosing of teachers who are versatile and can adjust to changing needs. It may very well be that in a given year more students will elect music literature than glee club. Or perhaps, at another time, a greater number of students will qualify for choir and that group will have to be rehearsed in two sections. Within recent years, with the growing popularity of folk and folk-rock songs, learning to play the guitar has become very popular. Have our instrumental instructors been able to add the teaching of the guitar to the schedule? It is important for teachers to see their place in a flexible, versatile, and ever broadening schedule.

Scheduling for the Many

The music program should never be placed in competition with other subjects for time in the roster. The best schedules are those which include activities performed before, during and after school hours. Theoretically, a student should be able to elect any musical offering. However, we must realize that some conflicts may arise because of the mechanics of rostering. Where this happens the best possible solution is the one which meets the greater need. It should be possible, however, to elect music courses with great ease and students should be encouraged to do so. The aim of the music educator is to reach as many students as possible.

Scheduling and the Length of the School Day

The length of the school day will most often determine how many subjects a student can elect. This varies throughout the country with school districts operating on a seven-, an eight-, or a nine-period schedule. A nine-period day will allow for more electives, and, as a result, for the establishment of a more diversified program. In working out the conflicts with academic subjects, those who work on the schedule find that the rostering is easiest when non-academic subjects are handled first. In a nine-period roster, music subjects which meet only one, two, or three periods per week can be scheduled with ease. The longer day does not handicap the election of special subjects, and it allows for two or three periods per day when all offerings do not vie for the same time in the schedule. This frees the necessary five periods per day for scheduling the academic majors. The time is coming when the nine-period day will be instituted in all schools. Until that time, schools which work on a shorter schedule will continue to use the zero period and make the eighth and ninth period after school an important part of the schedule.

Scheduling in the Large High School

In a large high school, with an enrollment of about 4,000 students, there may be three full-time vocal teachers and one full-time instrumental instructor. In addition, part-time, visiting instrumental teachers may be scheduled for instruction in brass, strings, woodwinds and percussion instruments. The roster for the staff should be flexible and may include the following electives:

Band—Marching and Symphonic
Orchestra
Small Instrumental Ensembles
Instrumental Instruction—All Band and Orchestral Instruments
Theory and the Essentials of Music
Harmony and Creative Music
Concert Choir
Vocal Ensembles
Voice Classes
Opera Workshop
Chorus—For all Twelfth-Grade Students—Preparation for singing at Graduation Exercises
General Music—Open to all Tenth-Grade Students
Music Appreciation
Music Literature
Clubs—Glee Clubs, Opera Club, Folk Music Club

The activities listed may be divided and scheduled for the four teachers. The normal school day, if it is seven periods long, is not too flexible. The music roster can then be lengthened to include a zero period, before school, and an eighth and ninth period for after-school activities. Music subjects can also be rostered over the three lunch periods, making it easier to resolve a conflict which may occur during those periods. Funds may be made available to compensate music teachers for extra hours of work.

Scheduling the Homeroom and the Assembly

Assemblies should be scheduled during the normal 20-minute homeroom period. The number of assemblies will be determined by the school population and the size of the auditorium. Assembly time may be extended as needed, and class time shortened by two to six minutes to compensate for the time. These assemblies can be scheduled and lengthened by making provisions for four sets of bell schedules:

(1) The regular 20-minute assembly.
(2) Increasing the assembly to half an hour, shortening all class periods for that day by two minutes.
(3) Increasing the assembly to 45 minutes by shortening all class periods for that day by four minutes
(4) Increasing the assembly to one hour by shortening all class periods for that day by six minutes.

Music teachers should be assigned to the assemblies to assist with the many scheduled programs. These teachers, therefore, should not be scheduled for homeroom assignments.

The roster for such a music department staff is shown in Figures 10–1 and 10–2.

Scheduling in the Small High School

In a small consolidated high school there may be two music teachers, one instrumental and the other vocal. The size of the school, in this case, will limit the number of music courses which can be offered. The schedule, however, may be flexible enough to meet the needs of the community. All music subjects, with the exception of general music, can be electives. The roster of activities can include:

A Cappella Choir
Band
Orchestra
Instrumental Instruction
General Music
Clubs

Limited teacher time will necessitate that music theory be taught as needed in the band, orchestra, instrumental instruction, and various choral activities. As the program grows there may be a possibility of hiring part-

CHORAL TEACHER I

PD.	MONDAY	TUESDAY	WEDNESDAY	THURSDAY	FRIDAY
0	CONCERT CHOIR ———————————————————————————→				
1	OFF PERIOD ———			————————→	
2	MUSIC LITERATURE	———————————————————→			
	HOMEROOM - ASSEMBLY —————————————				
3	12TH GRADE CHORUS (PREP. FOR GRADUATION)				
4	12TH GRADE CHORUS (PREP. FOR GRADUATION)				
5	LUNCH ——————————————————————————→				
6	HARMONY AND CREATIVE WORK ——————→				
7	OFF PERIOD ———————————————————————→				
8	VOICE CLASSES OPERA WORKSHOP	————————→		OPERA CLUB	VOICE CLASS
9	VOICE CLASSES OPERA WORKSHOP	————————→		VOICE CLASS	VOICE CLASS

Figure 10–1

CHORAL TEACHER II

PD.	MONDAY	TUESDAY	WEDNESDAY	THURSDAY	FRIDAY
0	VOCAL ENSEMBLE ⟶				
1	GENERAL MUSIC - 10TH GRADE ⟶				
2	OFF PERIOD ⟶				
	HOMEROOM - ASSEMBLY ⟶				
3	MUSIC THEORY AND CREATIVE WORK ⟶				
4	OFF PERIOD ⟶				
5	MUSIC APPRECIATION ⟶				
6	LUNCH ⟶				
7	GENERAL MUSIC - 10TH GRADE ⟶				
8	BOYS GLEE CLUB	GIRLS GLEE CLUB	FOLK MUSIC CLUB	BOYS GLEE CLUB	GIRLS GLEE CLUB

CHORAL TEACHER III

PD.	MONDAY	TUESDAY	WEDNESDAY	THURSDAY	FRIDAY
0	GLEE CLUB →				
1	GENERAL MUSIC - 10TH GRADE →				
2	12TH GRADE CHORUS (PREP. FOR GRADUATION) →				
	HOMEROOM - ASSEMBLY →				
3	OFF PERIOD →				
4	LUNCH →				
5	12TH GRADE CHORUS (PREP. FOR GRADUATION) →				
6	GENERAL MUSIC - 10TH GRADE →				
7	OFF PERIOD →				
8	ORGAN CLASS	MUSIC CLUB	ORGAN CLASS	MUSIC CLUB	ORGAN CLASS
9	↓	↓	↓	↓	↓

Figure 10–2

INSTRUMENTAL INSTRUCTOR

PD.	MONDAY	TUESDAY	WEDNESDAY	THURSDAY	FRIDAY
0	BAND ————————————————————————————→				
1	OFF PERIOD ——————————————————————→				
2	INSTRUMENTAL INSTRUCTION ————————→				
	HOMEROOM - ASSEMBLY ————————————				
3	INSTRUMENTAL INSTRUCTION ————————→				
4	LUNCH ———————————————————————————→				
5	INSTRUMENTAL INSTRUCTION ————————→				
6	INSTRUMENTAL ENSEMBLES ——————————→				
7	OFF PERIOD ——————————————————————→				
8	ORCHESTRA ———————————————————————→				
9	↓	↓	↓	↓	↓

time instrumental teachers who can release the full-time band and orchestra leader for other needed, regularly scheduled activities. Before- and after-school activities will be affected by the bus transportation of students. Each individual case will have to be scheduled so that students can get the greatest benefits from the school music program.

Where possible, the zero period in the morning may be reserved for related band activities, such as marching, drilling, and rehearsals for the half-time shows. The vocal teacher can also use the early morning period for small sectional rehearsals.

Suggested schedules for these teachers are listed in Figure 10–3.

Scheduling and the Computer

The development of the computer is revolutionizing the whole process of scheduling. The Music Educators National Conference has already issued materials dealing with data processing, programming, and the computer scheduling of music classes. It is a foregone conclusion that much good will come from the saving of administrative, supervisory, and teacher time. In those places where experimentation with high-speed computers has been going on, problems have resulted which need correcting. For one, the human element is eliminated from planning for the individual student; two, the lack of experienced computer technicians has made for many mistakes. No doubt, time and experience will overcome these obstacles. As we develop more experience with electronic scheduling it is to be hoped that more time will be available for the teacher to extend his preparation and teaching time.

Computer Help for an Integrated Curriculum

The number of courses which are listed in a given high school increases each year. A large high school today may offer as many as 200 different courses. Students are permitted to elect only five majors each year. It is obvious that the whole pattern for the education of our youth may have to change. A new approach which will involve the integration of subject matter seems to be suggested in the field of general education. The implications for music are tremendous. The revision of courses, with the integration of music and other subject fields, can bring about a better utilization of class time. Revising the courses and the course titles will take imagination and application. It is obvious that the advantages of the computerized system make it possible for pupil rosters to be processed promptly and teacher time to be best utilized.

VOCAL TEACHER

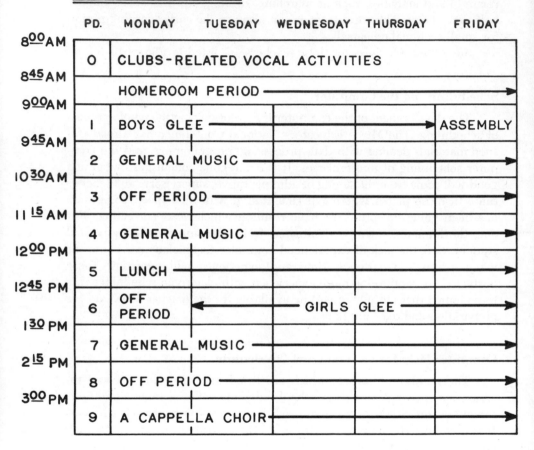

	PD.	MONDAY	TUESDAY	WEDNESDAY	THURSDAY	FRIDAY
8:00 AM	0	CLUBS-RELATED VOCAL ACTIVITIES				
8:45 AM		HOMEROOM PERIOD ———————————————→				
9:00 AM	1	BOYS GLEE ————————————————→				ASSEMBLY
9:45 AM	2	GENERAL MUSIC ———————————————————→				
10:30 AM	3	OFF PERIOD ———————————————————————→				
11:15 AM	4	GENERAL MUSIC ———————————————————→				
12:00 PM	5	LUNCH ———————————————————————————→				
12:45 PM	6	OFF PERIOD	←——————— GIRLS GLEE ———————————→			
1:30 PM	7	GENERAL MUSIC ———————————————————→				
2:15 PM	8	OFF PERIOD ———————————————————————→				
3:00 PM	9	A CAPPELLA CHOIR ————————————————→				

Figure 10–3

INSTRUMENTAL TEACHER

	PD.	MONDAY	TUESDAY	WEDNESDAY	THURSDAY	FRIDAY
8 00 AM	0	RELATED BAND ACTIVITIES-EXTRA REHEARSALS				
8 45 AM		HOMEROOM PERIOD ———————————————→				
9 00 AM	1	ORCHESTRA ——————————————→				ASSEMBLY
9 45 AM	2	OFF PERIOD ——————————————————→				
10 30 AM	3	INSTRUMENTAL INSTRUCTION ————————→				
11 15 AM	4	INSTRUMENTAL INSTRUCTION ————————→				
12 00 PM	5	LUNCH ————————————————————→				
12 45 PM	6	GENERAL MUSIC ——————————————→				
1 30 PM	7	INSTRUMENTAL INSTRUCTION ————————→				
2 15 PM	8	OFF PERIOD ——————————————————→				
3 00 PM	9	BAND ————————————————————→				

Scheduling for the Talented Student

In some schools the scheduling of students who plan to study music as a profession becomes a problem. It is desirable, of course, that such students begin to prepare themselves early. Every effort should be made in the high school for them to begin specializing. Classes, therefore, are scheduled in theory, harmony, the elements of music, sight singing, ear training, music literature, and applied music. After the basic requirements are met, most schools now permit students to make unlimited selection of courses. High school is the place for the general development of a broad educational background. Music educators should be in the forefront of the movement to produce well-informed and well-educated musicians. The schedule which the music teachers recommend for students must be flexible, practical, and adapted to meet current and future needs. Obviously, those who are talented will become musicians—professional or amateur. It is important, however, for them to see how relevant a knowledge of academic subjects is, in the career of a good musician and a well-educated personality. Music teachers must support a correct schedule for the individual student so that he graduates from high school well-equipped to face the future.

Scheduling for the Handicapped Child

We hear a great deal today about the education of handicapped children. Educators realize the importance of educating all people for participation in our society. Special schools have been set up for children with learning disabilities, underachievers, the retarded educable, the retarded trainable, and children with visual, auditory, and orthopedic handicaps. Music plays an important part in the education and habilitation of these children. Teachers who have been successful in this field have been especially trained to work with such students. Scheduling and working with handicapped students has been a rewarding experience for those teachers who have chosen to work in this field. While the scheduling of students whose work has been held up by their handicaps is difficult, the motivations which come with participation in a musical group have helped many of these boys and girls on to greater achievement in all subjects.

Scheduling for the Disadvantaged Student

Some families do not have the money to pay for musical instruments or the facilities for practicing at home. The school should make every effort to provide the instruments and schedule the pupils for the necessary practice periods, so that effective learning and growth are brought about. A flexible schedule, one adjusted to groups with special problems, can be designed to meet these needs. Students who are brought up in an environment of tension need the less rigid environment which comes with a short spontaneous singing period. A relaxing session of song singing can help pupils begin the school day in a positive manner. Appropriate and relevant assembly programs can be scheduled, so that pupils can learn about the importance of an education. Music, the morale builder, can be used to promote a cohesive group, a sense of belonging, and a feeling of worth.

Scheduling for Practice Rooms

Scheduling within the music department includes more than the assignment of teachers to the various courses and the rostering of students to these classes. With a limited number of classrooms, a schedule must be worked out so that there are no conflicts for the use of the practice rooms. Whenever possible, practice periods should be assigned on a regular, periodic basis. Each practice room should be equipped with a piano, record player, and a small desk or table for writing. A portable tape recorder should be available. Students should be encouraged to use the practice rooms, especially where various kinds of work will require privacy and quiet.

Progress in the technical and musical development of the student is based on daily, periodic practice. These working periods can be scheduled before school, after school, and during study periods. Where there are lunch periods of 45 minutes or longer, there is no reason why pupils cannot be assigned to practice during the lunch hour. Periods of assignment can be staggered without conflict and can be used to good advantage. In a large crowded school, many students will look to the practice room as a refuge from the congestion of the lunchroom, as a period of relaxation and enjoyment, and also as an opportunity for further musical study. Maximum use of the facilities should be encouraged.

Earning Carnegie Units

Just as a student receives Carnegie Units for English, science, mathematics and social studies he can receive units for the study of music. A Carnegie Unit is granted for 120 hours of attendance in a class for a whole school year. The State of Pennsylvania, for example, requires that 12 Carnegie Units be earned for a high school diploma. They are divided as follows:

	English	3
Required 7	History	2 (Including Pennsylvania History)
	Mathematics	1
	Science	1
	Physical Education	
	Music	
Electives 5	Art	
	Foreign Language	
	Home Arts	
	Shops	

Total   12 (Required for graduation)

At least four of these Carnegie Units can be taken in music. Those subjects chosen could be theory (1), harmony (2) and music literature (1). Another schedule might include the a cappella choir, band, or orchestra, with three Units granted for a three-year period, plus music appreciation for one year. This will prepare a student for specialization at a college or conservatory. It is the individually planned schedule, one which meets the needs of the pupil, that is important. Credit can be granted for work achieved.

Scheduling Activities for Little or No Credit

There are many activities existing within a music curriculum that have little to do with the awarding of credit. The situation is best left that way. Many students who elect to join a music group do not necessarily join for credit. In most cases, participating in these activities has its own rewards, and credits may be eliminated. Where credit is needed, however, it should be granted. In one high school where the granting of credit was revised, pupils were permitted to attend choir with no credit. The students were delighted. Each one now was able to elect an additional academic subject such as a language, a course in science, or one in mathematics. Where a student chose to elect the academic-music curriculum, however, choir, band, orchestra, theory, harmony, and music literature courses were to be taken for major credit. All other students could elect the same subjects for no credit, on a pass-fail basis, and thereby did not jeopardize the opportunity to choose another academic subject which was needed or desirable.

Devising Other Motivations

Enrolling in other music activities, which is based on specialized motivation and interest, need not always be rewarded by the granting of credit. In fact, one could say that the real test of student interest in these activities would be removal of tangible rewards and observing how many still want to participate. The granting of credit is usually the lesser motivation for participation in music activities. True, credit should be given where needed, but the importance of credit as motivation is greatly overestimated. The music teacher should be free to use credit to the best advantage of the students.

Granting Honor Points

In many schools, the student government grants a specific number of honor points towards a certificate for contributing to the cultural life of the school. These points are awarded for participating in approved school activities after school hours. Many school musical organizations practice for additional hours before and after school, play concerts, take part in parades and pageants, and thereby earn honor points toward a certificate. When a pupil has accumulated a specific number of hours, he receives a certificate of merit and a pin. Sometimes a student receives a bronze pin for accumulating 100 points, a silver pin for 200 points, and a gold pin for totalling 300 points or more. This, then, is another form of recognition and high school students wear their pins proudly.

The scheduling and granting of credit is a much more complicated subject than the combined presentation made here. With the advent of the computer, texts dealing exclusively with the problems of the roster and the advisability of granting credit through Carnegie Units are in the offing. It is to be hoped that with these new developments the schedule will become more flexible and the rewards for participation in a music curriculum will include the granting of credits as needed. It is also desirable for the scheduling of musical activities to go beyond the mechanics involved and make each activity rewarding in itself.

Eleven

Developing the
Music Teacher

The development of a coordinated, integrated curriculum should lead to an effective interaction of the various staff members. Often, however, where we find a wide variety of musical courses, the many offerings can be totally unrelated to each other. There may be a good relationship among the staff members, and teachers may present good individual programs, but this does not necessarily create the setting for an organic curriculum. The development of the teachers and the courses into an integrated program is of paramount importance. The better the interaction and coordination of the staff, the better the quality of the music program.

Choosing the Teacher

Before we can involve the teacher in a coordinated program, we must evaluate him to see how he can take his place in the schedule. First, he must learn quickly how to handle and teach students of high school age. He must have a working knowledge of adolescent psychology and be able to sell what he has to offer. His background should include adequate professional training, the ability to demonstrate skills which he is teaching, and certification which will indicate proper preparation in the arts, sciences, and humanities. His appearance, speech, tone of voice, and positive personality are tools which should command the respect of the students. The teacher should be selected, then, with consideration for the diversified needs of a curriculum, and the way in which the contribution which he has to make can best be used.

Developing Teacher Philosophy and Goals

Aims and objectives have changed through the years. The philosophy sets the goals, and we must have a clear idea of how and where we are going. All teachers should be in agreement with the basic aims and objectives as set forth by the staff in a given school. There should always be opportunities for new ideas, devices, experimentation, and honest dissent. We should never lose sight of what musical performance and music listening is doing to and for students. The organic staff development, through the growth of a philosophy, become extremely important in that it helps the teachers to set goals from the beginning and is flexible enough to change with new needs.

Developing a Positive Personality

Personality is an important factor in developing rapport between teachers and students. Friendliness, cooperative spirit, good humor, and enthusiasm help to bridge the gap between young people and their instructors. High school teachers must build an understanding of adolescents, based on a full awareness of how young people grow and behave in this formative period of their lives. The security of the teacher himself can affect his personality. One who is emotionally secure in his job and in his relationships with other teachers, the administration, and the community is more likely to develop a positive personality. Administrators who establish an atmosphere of security in their schools help teachers to relax and concentrate on the work at hand.

The music itself can be used in the development of personality. In learning to respond to music, one can become sensitized to the whole subject of human feelings and behavior. The moods caught by the composers in their compositions are good examples of how a sensitive human being felt at that particular moment when he wrote or recorded the sounds. This, however, requires some direction from teachers. There is a common misconception about those who participate in musical activities. It is generally felt that music has a magic charm in that it transforms all children and adults into saintly individuals. Nothing can be further from the truth. Temperamental musicians are noted for their tantrums, and there have been public exhibitions of cantankerous behavior. In order to be able to teach effectively one must be able to relate to people. A pleasing personality is one of the greatest assets that a teacher can develop. It is to be hoped that teacher-training institutions and in-service training courses will spend more time in the development of teacher personality.

Developing Relationships with Students

Teachers must continue to develop and expand their backgrounds in music and related fields. In addition, courses in psychology can help with an understanding of adolescent behavior. Creating an atmosphere of relaxation in the classroom assists the teacher in building good relationships. A feeling of interest and friendship between teachers and students can be a tremendous asset. The function of the teacher is clearly defined. He must communicate knowledge in a systematic, good-humored manner, so that the pupil will want to continue on his own. He must develop patience and understanding and at times must be able to use firmness. Anything which upsets the relationship will tend to detract from the disciplines necessary for learning.

Setting Up Classroom Procedures and Disciplines

The presentation of subject matter is more successful when teachers have mastered the technics of proper classroom management. The recording of attendance and lateness and the distribution of supplies, books, and materials are only a few of the chores which a teacher performs. These must become routine so that only a minimum of time is taken from the actual teaching. Large music classes require seating charts which help with the organization of each class. The ability to take the roll in two or three minutes by just checking the empty seats indicates a well-organized teacher. All discussions concerning absence, lateness, or seating can be taken care of before or after class. Nothing must interfere with the time set aside for classroom work. Periods of relaxation can be built into the teaching sessions, but a reasonable attempt should be made to complete the business of the day. High school students have pressing needs. If not taught habits of self-discipline they will tend to become lax in meeting classroom obligations. The disorganized teacher often is bogged down by poorly handled routines, and small deviations from the norm by students will tend to accumulate. These can then develop into a series of disciplinary problems. Advance planning for the handling of classroom procedures will pay off.

Preparing Seating Plans

There are several types of seating plans which music teachers can use in the various classes for which they are scheduled. The usual practice is to draw the placement arrangement on graph paper in pencil, allowing for changes which must be made from time to time. A choir, of course, is arranged by voices and of necessity individuals are shifted periodically. Theory and harmony classes are usually grouped by ability and state of advancement. General music classes can be seated by voice parts or in alphabetical order, depending upon what activities the teacher is planning to conduct.

The seating plan for each class is extremely important, and the seating chart takes on special significance. It enrolls the students on the first day and sets the scene immediately for the year's work. A Chorus 4 class, which is set up to prepare for singing in four parts at the graduation exercises, finds out immediately why it is there. The teacher builds self-discipline in the students by holding out the task to be accomplished as a desirable end toward which the group will work. Although the Chorus 4 classes will spend a whole year on this work, the motivations are set up from the first day. The class will not only learn the music for the commencement ceremonies; they will also learn how to read music, use their voices more effectively, develop a repertoire of choral songs, listen to recordings of other mass choirs, and in general develop a better understanding of music and musicianship. The seating plan, set up on the first day, helps the teacher to get things off to a good start.

There are several commercial companies which put out classroom seating charts in which student attendance cards can be inserted. These systems are flexible in that cards can be removed if a student is dropped or shifted or if the teacher chooses to move individuals or rearrange the seating of the class. Roll can be taken quickly in this way. The individual student card can be made up to resemble the sample shown in Figure 11–1.

Directions for Using Seating Chart Cards

A card should be filled in by each student. The teacher should pass through the aisles, collect the completed cards, and insert them in the seating chart as seats are assigned. This prepares a seating arrangement on the first day in which the class reports to the music room.

On a day in which a student is absent, the teacher records the date. If the student is late, the teacher may draw a diagonal line across the date. Where a student has cut the class a red horizontal line through the date can be used. On dates when students are present, space can be used to enter marks for classroom participation or any other accomplishment. Teachers may invent their own codes for recording what happens in each class.

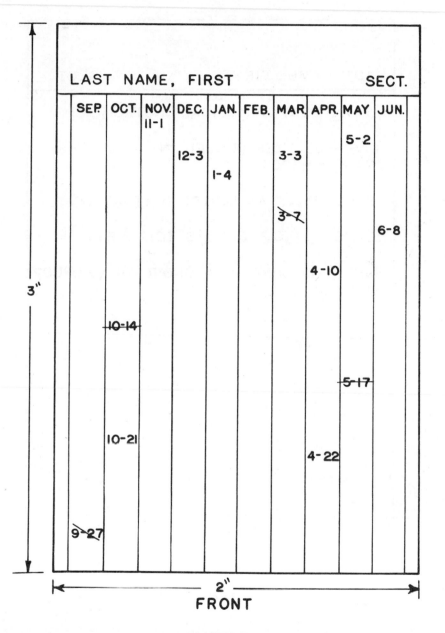

Figure 11–1

LAST NAME, FIRST	SECT.

DO YOU PLAY A MUSICAL INSTRUMENT?

HAVE YOU EVER PLAYED IN AN ORCHES-
TRA? WHERE?

DO YOU HAVE AN INSTRUMENT AT HOME?

DO YOU SING? S A T B (CIRCLE)

HAVE YOU SUNG IN A CHOIR OR CHORUS?
WHERE?

BACK

When cards are inserted in the seating chart, the complete class roll will look like that shown in Figure 11–2.

It is a difficult job to make up these seating charts by hand, although some teachers have been known to do it. Once they are available, however, they are semi-permanent and can be used over and over again. If teachers find it difficult to purchase these charts, they should find a means of constructing them, as they play an important part in the organization of the classroom.

Assigning Homework

An area in which teacher-pupil relationships breaks down is in the planning for homework. Developing the technics for being brief, concise, and specific is important in the making of assignments. Teachers should state very clearly what they want students to do. In a high school music literature class a music teacher said. "Today, we begin to study the operas of Puccini. Your weekly assignment, which is due on Friday, will be for you to write a brief paper on the contribution of Giacomo Puccini to the field of opera." The class seemed confused. Hands of the class members moved upward. There were the usual questions: "How do you spell his name?" "Was he Italian—his name sounds Italian?" "Do you want a biography in the paper?" "Shall we list all of his operas or just the important ones?" Much of this confusion could have been avoided. Italian, German, French, and Russian names of composers are at best difficult to spell. Students with a minimum background in music history and literature can become confused in a maze of paper writing. If the teacher wants the pupils to do the necessary research, the wording of the assignment on the blackboard becomes important. "Your assignment for this week is 'The Contribution of Giacomo Puccini to the Development of Opera.' List the important operas of Puccini in chronological order. That is how we are going to study them in class. A brief biography of the composer should be included at the beginning of the paper. Are there any questions?"

Developing Teacher Communication

Each teacher, no doubt, builds his own "bag of tricks," but these devices are only a means to an end. They are not a substitute for the subject matter which is to be taught, or for bona-fide teacher-pupil rapport. The accumulation of materials and devices and subject matter then adds up to the curriculum which becomes the sum total of musical experiences in the classroom. Teachers should continue to work to refine relationships with their pupils and to build avenues of communication which will lead to more effective learning.

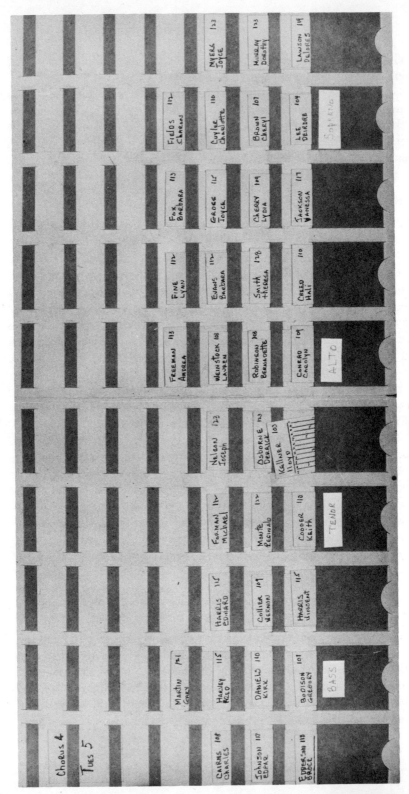

Figure 11-2

The question is often raised as to how effective are some of our modern approaches to the teaching of music. We have all seen teachers use a most conservative approach and achieve excellent results. We have also seen unusual psychological approaches in which teaching is most successful. In the final analysis, the success of instruction is measured by how well the pupils learn what the teacher presents in class. Each teacher must work within the context of his own personality and background, to develop the many ways in which good learning situations can be established.

Developing Resourcefulness

The music teacher must be resourceful as the needs for subject matter and skills are constantly changing. He must periodically look at the curriculum to evaluate its relevancy. Within recent years, for example, a major revolution has been taking place in the field of music composition. Do our traditional methods for the teaching of music theory, harmony, and composition remain unchanged? All about us we witness the development of new technics in the field of popular music. Creative musicians are learning to use the Row Series. Developments in electronics have also brought us the Moog Synthesizer. Do we involve students with the inventiveness of modern composers? The music teacher must be a resource person. He should have a healthy interest in and knowledge of all musical developments. He need not become a walking encyclopedia, but together with his students he can explore newly developed areas in the field.

Specialists in music education must also recognize the importance of utilizing knowledge in the field of electronics. In all of the listening courses the teacher uses stereo record players, stereo tape, and the modern sound motion picture projector. In choral and instrumental classes there are stereo tape recorders, electronic tuning devices, stroboscopes, the strobotuner, and the stroboconn. Recent developments in sound videotape holds out new promise for music education. Now entire specialized lessons can be prepared on teletape which can be kept on a reserve shelf and used as needed. The developing teacher must learn to use all of these devices to enrich the backgrounds of the students.

Developing Relationships with Administrators

Music teachers and administrators should develop a rapport and work toward common goals. In a large school system, there are department heads, supervisors, directors, principals, vice principals, district superintendents, associate superintendents and the superintendent of schools. In most cases, the music teacher deals directly with a department head, a supervisor, or a principal. A large urban school is very much like a small town, with the principal acting as the mayor and the department heads serving as members of his cabinet. The problems of health, security, community relations, and budgeting must be considered in addition to educational problems. The principal, who focuses on the entire program, must help create an atmosphere in which learning can take place. While it is true that musical activities benefit most of the students, music teachers should be reasonable in making requests for special consideration. Administrators, generally, are interested in music education and are cooperative, especially where the curriculum meets the needs of a large number of students.

The amount of money appropriated for a music curriculum will depend to a large extent upon the relationship between teachers and administrators. Music educators have an obligation to keep superiors informed as to the latest developments in the field. Sometimes a music teacher may work very closely with a supervisor. In a number of communities the senior high school music teacher is also the music supervisor in the elementary schools. Developing good relationships with all administrators and supervisors is important in that communications are kept open for interpreting the program. Where there is agreement as to curricula, courses of study, technics, and how to approach the various aspects of the program, relationships can be maintained on a high professional level. It is just as important for the teacher to indoctrinate the supervisor as it is for the supervisor to change the approach of the teacher. If all communication is kept on a professional level, differences can be resolved in favor of trying new technics, materials, and approaches. Teachers should be permitted sufficient opportunities to experiment with advanced ideas, provided that procedures and results can be evaluated periodically. Where communications are kept open, teachers and administrators can objectively evaluate the program so that it can be enlarged and strengthened as needed.

Developing Relationships with Parents and the Community

Teachers must also develop proper relationships with parents. Most parents have the same objectives for their children as the teachers have. There is a great deal to be gained from involving parents in planning for students. Conferences concerning whether a student should work toward a professional career or seek amateur status as a musician are important. Parents, who should play a part in the making of decisions, have confidence in the advice of the music educator when they feel his concern for the talent, needs, and integrity of the student. Meetings which lead to better rapport can also work towards better community support for the program. Invitations to concerts, recitals, outdoor programs, and other community-wide activities involve parents and the community. By inviting the public into the school we take our first steps towards building good relationships. The growth and development of the music teacher should include the opportunity to set up these connections with parents and the community.

Most parents are directly interested in their schools, first, because their children spend a minimum of six hours a day there and second, because they pay the bill for the operation of the schools. They want a balanced educational program through which their children can grow intellectually. Some of them may question the value of music in the curriculum. Interpreting the value of music in the general education program for parents and the community is not too difficult. The music teacher is in an enviable position. Much of what he accomplishes can be displayed in public. Programs which are offered to the community can do much to interpret the curriculum. If the music teacher develops a philosophy and a program which shows the value of a music education, parents and the community will speak up for the program when support is needed.

Joining Professional Organizations

An important resource for the development of the teachers is the wide variety of professional organizations which they may join. The *Music Educators Journal,* the official organ of the Music Educators National Conference, is a major source for keeping up with the latest developments in the field. General education and music education conferences provide an opportunity to learn about new and experimental ideas and programs which teachers can use. Exhibits and demonstrations present new materials and methods which are of practical use for teachers. These meetings, organized on a state and regional basis, are available in all parts of the United States. Teachers can learn much from these professional contacts.

Developing Teacher Morale

All teacher talent should be utilized for the improvement of the program. When the teacher learns new skills or reinforces old ones he can make an increased contribution to the staff and the musical life of the school. One who sees the need for learning to "bandstrate" a new arrangement for the dance or stage band, and can teach students to make similar ones, will find the results rewarding. Teacher morale improves with the awareness of contributing to the program as the need arises.

Opportunities are always presenting themselves for experimenting with new ideas which require the development of new skills. Progress in a given area and success in general will give greater satisfaction to the instructor who is willing to learn.

Teacher morale is also improved by being given the opportunity to work at the things which they do best. Sometimes a teacher is called upon to teach a subject for which he is not qualified. If there is a staff of skilled music teachers it should not be difficult to assign the various courses so that subjects are taught by those prepared to teach them. There is no point to asking a choral teacher to teach a class in theory and harmony if he is not prepared to do so. It is not only bad for teacher morale; it also means that students will not receive the best instruction. Where the staff is small and there are fewer alternatives, however, every effort should be made by the teacher to develop the new skills necessary for effective teaching.

Teacher morale comes also from developing the ability to measure and evaluate his effectiveness in the classroom. An instructor should be able to test to find out how well the students learn what he sets out to teach. In the end, we judge a teacher by what he teaches—not by his methods, his procedures, his material, his manner, or his personality. True, all of these things are important, but in the final analysis the test is: How well did the students learn? Even if the results of such examination are poor, the morale of the teacher will go up as he attempts to do something about it. If he works at improvement, he will set up a revised program through which students can learn.

Working conditions often affect the morale of teachers. If the facilities are poor acoustically, and the music activities disturb other classrooms and teachers, the music teacher is confronted with problems which affect his ability to communicate with others. When the equipment is old and obsolete, and breaks down regularly, teaching is affected. Poor record players and pianos which are beyond repair or the lack of blackout shades to darken a room for the showing of slides, films, and teletapes can dampen the ardor of an instructor. Every effort should be made by administrators to provide equipment and facilities which are adequate. The morale of the teacher and the success of the program depend upon it.

Opportunities should be provided for music teachers to serve on committees within the general education program. The writing of curriculum materials must not be relegated to the department chairmen only, or to any one member of the staff. If each developing teacher is a specialist in his own field, he becomes the logical one to write that particular contribution to the curriculum. If there are two or three choral specialists, they can work together to evolve a course of study which in their combined judgment is workable. Where the music department is presenting a program entitled "A Night at the Opera," the teacher or teachers who are specialists in this area are the logical ones to outline and direct it. Dividing the responsibility for carrying through a broad program can lead to higher morale within the department. Teachers must develop a sense of belonging.

The orchestral assistant who goes to as many sectional rehearsals of a city-wide ensemble as he can, and is familiar with the music and the students, can step in at any time to conduct the group. How well he sees himself as a part of the team is important to him. There is a great need for the highly specialized teacher. There is also a great need for teachers who are versatile. The happiest ones are those who find satisfaction in making a contribution which is important to the program. Higher morale comes with teacher and student involvement, accomplishment, and recognition.

In short, teacher development and morale will be determined, to a great extent, by helping music teachers to find their place in the entire curriculum. The relationship of music teachers with other teachers, the administration, and the community will be good if the part which music plays in the general curriculum is properly interpreted and understood. Freedom to grow, develop, experience, and experiment will result in an improved program of instruction for the students and a high morale for the music department staff.

Twelve

Evaluating and Organizing Facilities, Equipment, and Materials

Planning for new or revised facilities, equipment, and materials is an important part of the music educator's work. Periodically, tools and facilities for learning must be replaced or changed in order to keep up with new developments in the field. Large school systems have special administrative departments which have the overall responsibility for researching and organizing these facilities. Smaller school systems must depend upon the resources within the schools and consultants who are brought in to make recommendations and plans.

Involving Music Teachers in the Planning

Where administrators are responsible and progressive, the music educators are consulted in the making of plans. While it is true that an architect who is a specialist in school construction will be familiar with general practices in the field, the advice of music teachers who know what the needs are can be invaluable. Teachers are more familiar with the kinds of equipment which are needed. The placement of bulletin boards, blackboards, electrical outlets, and seats is usually left to the discretion of the teacher who will be using the facilities.

Where to situate the music suite in the school building is extremely important to teachers and students. In making preparations for the construction of a new high school, for example, a very elaborate and well-planned music suite was placed on the third floor of a distant wing. The music teachers, if consulted, would have asked that the classrooms be located adjacent to the school auditorium, which is the scene of most concert performances. Transporting musical instruments, stands, platforms, band uniforms and choir robes, becomes a major project when classrooms and storage rooms are far removed from the auditorium. When decisions such as these are to be made, music teachers should be among the planners. Administrators are increasingly consulting teachers in order to arrive at the most effective facilities for music instruction.

Using Source Materials and References

An excellent source for the development of teacher background in the planning of music facilities is the book *Music, Buildings, Rooms and Equipment*, which is distributed by the NEA Publication Sales, 1201 Sixteenth Street NW, Washington, D. C. 20036. Prepared by the Music Educators National Conference, it presents in great detail plans for schools of all sizes and shapes. Facilities from programs which utilize the services of only one teacher, to those which include a large, well-integrated staff, are shown. Much information is available on this subject. Additional, new materials can be secured by writing to the Music Educators National Conference. In this chapter one can only make a few important proposals and suggest other sources for reference and information.

Building All-Purpose Rooms

If music teachers are to play an important part in preparations, they must come to the planning meetings with specific ideas which will lead to the construction of functional facilities. Many music rooms cost more to build than the average classroom. School boards and taxpayers will insist on a full-time use of these facilities. A large choral rehearsal room, which serves the choir and the vocal ensemble for only two periods a day, can be planned to house general music classes and music appreciation classes as well and can also serve as a small lecture hall. With blackout shades, the room can easily be converted into a visual aid room where films and slide lectures can be presented. In an ever—expanding and flexible program, the music department should make every effort to utilize the facilities full time. All rooms should be planned and equipped so that a variety of music activities can be conducted in each one.

Teachers should not be expected to work out all of the scientific, artistic, and budgetary details involved in the construction of music rooms. They should be involved, however, in the planning so that the facilities, when completed, will be acoustically treated, well-lighted, well-ventilated, and of sufficient size to accommodate the rehearsals of large combined mass activities. Music instructors can be a great help to administrators and architects who are ultimately responsible for plans and construction. The planning committee will want to have these specific questions answered:

(1) How many students in the school will be scheduled for music classes? What kind of classes?
(2) How many teachers will the budget allow?
(3) Will the budget permit a complete and separate building, a floor or section of a new building, or will it be necessary to remodel existing facilities?
(4) Where can the facilities be located? Near the auditorium, in a place removed from the main building, or in a wing where they do not interfere with other school activities?
(5) Will all of the equipment be new or will any of it be moved from the older facilities?

Planning the Auditorium

The auditorium stage should be planned large enough to seat, or to place standing, large combined classes and instrumental ensembles. Where this is not possible, it should be feasible to plan for the use of the stage and the pit to accommodate large numbers of students. Here, with the use of choir stands, groups can be arranged on various levels, on the stage and in the pit, behind the orchestra in the pit, and on the floor level, to make for a massing of all participating groups in a festival. The stage also should have a variety of electrical and sound outlets for utilizing light and audio equipment. Overhead, hanging microphones should be available. Procenium lights, footlights, floodlights, and spots should be built into the stage facilities in order to dramatize all presentations more effectively. The school auditorium, and its stage, which in many cases will be the only large meeting and concert hall in the community, should be equipped to serve the school during the day and the school and community in the evening. Every effort should be made to create a modern, practical, functional, and well-equipped meeting hall, one which will meet present and future needs.

The space in front of the stage, which is normally called the orchestra pit, should serve many purposes. It should be planned to seat a large or small chorus, and a large or small band or orchestra. Appropriate jacks and outlets for electricity, microphones, and the electronic organ should

Figure 12–1: The auditorium stage should be planned to accommodate large and small groups and should be flexible enough to meet varying

be built into the plans. Access to the stage from the pit should be arranged so that groups can move up and down the side stairs without crowding. Easy entrance to the stage from the rear is also important. Electrical and sound outlets should be planned at various spots on the auditorium floor, so that slide projectors, motion picture projectors, and microphones can be plugged in as needed with a minimum use of extension cords.

Great consideration should be given to auditorium seating. This should be planned in accordance with student numbers and community needs. The larger the number of square feet built into the auditorium, the more expensive the project becomes. If the planners keep in mind the diverse uses of the facility, the size of the hall can be determined by the number of functions that it serves. Special care should be taken not to make the auditorium too large. While community needs must be taken into consideration, it is being constructed primarily for educational purposes. If the seating is planned for assembly and festival use, it will be adequate for adult education and community activities. Architects who are specialists in planning for educational institutions are well prepared to solve this problem.

The auditorium, whether it is new or being remodeled, should be acoustically soundproofed; it should be air conditioned and carpeted. The costs of these items are small when compared to the overall budget for the construction. Massing large groups of students and members of the community for assemblies and festivals demands a temperature control system which will make the hall useful all year. There are many occasions in which the entire school meets together for a variety of programs. Learning is encouraged under conditions of comfort. Treating the auditorium acoustically is important if the students are to hear themselves in rehearsal or present their programs effectively. Tape recordings, both for sound and closed-circuit television, are poor where the reverberation and absorption are not adjusted acoustically. The modern school uses the newest information and materials in building the school plant. An excellent source of information for the scientific treatment of music facilities is: *Acoustical Environment of School Buildings*, Technical Report No. 1. New York: Educational Facilities Laboratories, Inc., 1963.

Locating the Music Department Quarters

The logical place to locate the music rooms is adjacent to the auditorium, the most important scene for displaying the work of the music department. Some school systems have housed the program in a separate building, but in these cases the theatre or auditorium is usually placed in the same structure. The various areas set aside for rehearsals, music listening classes, and practice rooms should be arranged so that pupils have easy access to the facilities. Soundproofing should be built into the entire area with walls, ceilings, and floors treated for the best acoustical results. This is important for two reasons: first, because other classes in the school should not be disturbed by sounds emanating from the music wing; and second, because music students should study in facilities which permit them to hear the music which they create without any distortion. Placing the music suite far away from the remainder of the school is not always the answer. Planning it to be housed behind or adjacent to the auditorium is perhaps a better solution to the problem.

Planning the Size of Classrooms

Room size cannot be determined by the number of students enrolled in a school. It is determined, rather, by the number of pupils planned for an activity. While a 100-voice choir may exist in a large metropolitan high school, it is also likely to be found in a smaller, rural consolidated school. It is safe to say that in planning a band or orchestra room 20 to 25 square feet per student should be allowed, so that a 90-piece instrumental unit should have a floor plan of approximately 2,000 square feet of floor space. A classroom for choral groups can be planned far more easily. In a rehearsal room where risers will not be used, 15 square feet per student can be allowed. For a 100-voice choir, then, no less than 15 square feet per pupil will be needed for the rehearsal room. Where risers are used, an elevation of eight inches and a depth of 40 inches will be adequate for the room. Here, 18 to 20 square feet per person should be used as a scale. Thus, a minimum of 2,000 square feet will be needed for this type of room.

Setting the Ceiling Level

In making plans for rooms which will not resound with massive reverberations, the height of the room is important. The average height of eight- to ten-foot ceilings will prove to be totally inadequate. Ceilings approximately 15 feet high are infinitely better for a choir room which will seat 100 singers comfortably. High ceilings have another advantage; windows can be placed higher bringing in better light and providing for more adequate ventilation. When the ceiling is high and risers are planned for the elevated seating of choristers, the acoustically conditioned sound will tend to encourage active listening and the more effective blending of the voices. A room built in this manner also will tend to become a better studio for recording the band or orchestra, or any choral group. The

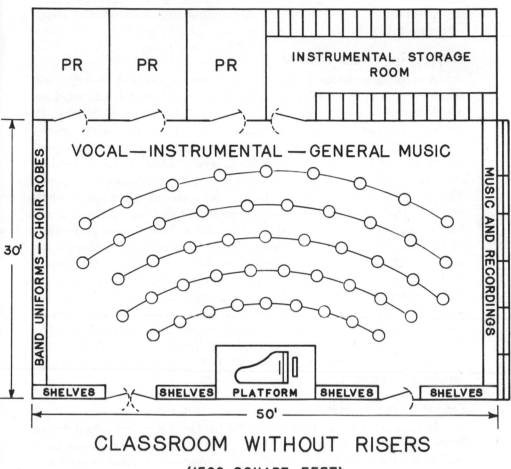

CLASSROOM WITHOUT RISERS

(1500 SQUARE FEET)

Figure 12–2

reverberation and distortion level can be reduced to a minimum and the absorption adjusted to the needs of all performing groups. The philosophy of the music education program should be built into the facilities. Above all, the new rooms and the equipment should help students to become more musical.

Planning for Proper Lighting

A music room which is planned for maximum use and flexibility will require proper lighting. With a ceiling which is 15 feet high and windows which are placed high, special attention must be given to lighting. Illumination engineers will have to take into consideration all of the special reading problems which differentiate between the reading of music and the reading of printed words in a book. The reading of music involves printing which is usually poorer than that found in an ordinary text book. The paper is usually of inferior quality and many of the music symbols are small and can be seen only with difficulty. Well-planned lighting will tend to encourage accurate music reading and will discourage performing by ear. Students who sit on different levels will experience differing degrees of light depending upon how close they are to the sources of the illumination. Again, lighting engineers will have to consider where to place the lighting fixtures so that the contrast and brightness ratios between the ceiling fixtures, the music stands, and the printed page in books being read are sufficient to provide proper illumination levels. *The Illuminating Engineering Society Lighting Handbook* published by the Illuminating Engineering Society in 1952 in New York can serve as a guide for planning the lighting in a new music suite.

Planning the Choral Room

In planning for the choral room we must face up to problems different from those of the instrumental room. Most modern choral rooms have built into their facilities risers which are so arranged that the choral director can easily check on posture, diction, balance, correct part singing, and disciplinary problems. With each riser elevated six to eight inches, singers can have an unobstructed view and can more easily follow the directions of the conductor. If each riser has a depth of approximately 40 inches, a passageway in front of each row of chairs allows for adherence to any safety regulations which may exist. Several temporary aisles may be made to allow for division by voices. Thus the choral conductor can also be permitted to walk up and down the open spaces to check on intonation, voice production, correct part singing, or posture. Actually, in performance the choir does not use the aisles. The ranks can be closed by coming together

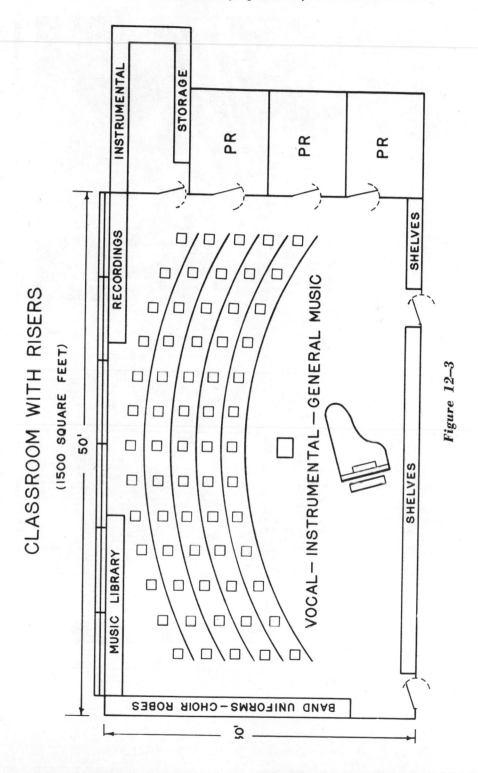

CLASSROOM WITH RISERS

(1500 SQUARE FEET)

INSTRUMENTAL

STORAGE

PR

PR

PR

RECORDINGS

SHELVES

VOCAL — INSTRUMENTAL — GENERAL MUSIC

MUSIC LIBRARY

SHELVES

BAND UNIFORMS—CHOIR ROBES

50'

Figure 12–3

Figure 12–4: The modern choral room should have built into its facilities conditions which duplicate those in actual performance and should also be flexible enough for the conducting of a variety of musical activities

Helen M. Bauhof, 352 Church Lane, Philadelphia, Pa. 19144

and eliminating the passageways as the group stands for a concert program.

Using a Flexible Seating Plan

In these days of soundproofed and carpeted choral practice rooms, there is little advantage to fixed theatre chairs for use during rehearsals. Some conductors prefer benches to chairs. During the rehearsal choir members may sit temporarily, but most of the time they practice in a standing position. Since the choral room is bound to be an all-purpose room, it is best, perhaps, to use modern drop-tablet armchairs, with the arms out of sight except in those classes where note-taking and written tests are used as a part of the instruction. These facilities will allow for singing with good posture in a seated position, or standing for rehearsals as the various disciplines are required. It is better to have a flexible arrangement with the chairs movable and used as needed. Often this tiered room can serve as a small recital hall. Extra chairs can be brought in to the riser section where the audience can sit, while individual soloists and smaller ensembles can perform from the flat lower level. A flexible seating system will allow for greater versatility in the program.

Providing Musical Equipment

The choral practice room should have a fine piano, an organ, and provisions for the use of a stereo record player and tape recorder. In planning these facilities, up-to-date equipment should be selected to present an effective production and reproduction of sound. The modern tape recorder is a boon to the choral conductor. In a few moments, students can hear themselves as they really sound and corrections can be made quickly. Hearing how a world-famous choral group sings the composition which the choir is studying often motivates a group to do its best work. In the music department the piano is in constant use. It must be sturdy and well tuned in order to maintain its pitch. In choosing a piano for the choral room, it is mandatory that the planners select an excellent, well-built instrument.

Planning the Orchestra and Band Room

The orchestra and band room should also be built with facilities which lend themselves to great flexibility. There are differences of opinion concerning the advisability of using permanent risers which are, in themselves, flexible. The trend now seems to be towards furnishing a large room with portable risers which can be moved about at will and used in sections to meet the needs of all types of instrumental groups. These can

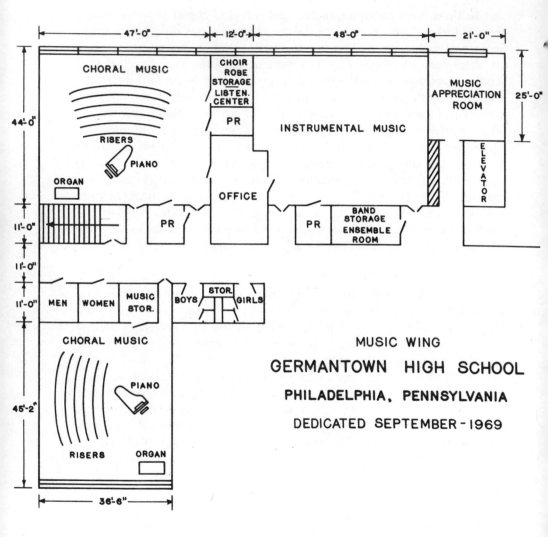

MUSIC WING
GERMANTOWN HIGH SCHOOL
PHILADELPHIA, PENNSYLVANIA
DEDICATED SEPTEMBER - 1969

Figure 12–5

be transported to the auditorium, to outdoor band concerts, to a park, or to any hall in the community. Commercial manufacturers of risers build a variety of elevations in various styles and shapes. Many schools with generous budgets purchase a separate set of risers for the auditorium so that the platforms are not moved around too much. In any case, portable risers seem to answer the question of flexibility for the band and orchestra room.

The various positions in which these risers are arranged can allow for the conductor to see all of the members of the orchestra or band. Straight-backed chairs should be used for correct posture and vision. If the conductor's podium is elevated, he can be seen without difficulty by all the musicians. The music stands should be made of a light, sturdy metal and should rest on a firm base so that they do not fall over easily. A good piano and an electronic organ should be included in plans for this room.

Planning the Practice Rooms

Practice rooms should be placed close to the instrumental and choral rooms. The number included should be determined by need, and they should be designed for before-school, during-school, and after-school use. Where students have an opportunity to practice at home, this study should be encouraged. In many of the big city music departments, especially where students are underprivileged, opportunities should be provided for potential musicians to practice in school. Use of the practice rooms should be scheduled and whenever possible teachers should check to see how the pupils are progressing.

The size of the practice rooms will vary with the needs, but most music educators will recommend no less than 75 square feet for the floor area. Although it is not necessary to have a small piano in each room, it is desirable, for the benefit of practicing pianists and accompanists, to include them in all rooms if the budget will allow it. The room should also include a record player, a small table for writing, and easy access to a tape recorder.

Much teaching can go on in the practice rooms. If small ensemble practicing rooms are included in the plans, chamber music groups, vocal duets, trios, and quartets can be rehearsed without involving a large classroom which can be used for other purposes. Auditions and conferences with theory, harmony and composition students can all be held in practice rooms.

Planning Facilities for a Small Music Department

For a small music department, a large, all-purpose room should be

Figure 12–6: The orchestra and band room should be planned with facilities which lend themselves to great flexibility

Helen M. Bauhof, 352 Church Lane, Philadelphia, Pa. 19144

Helen M. Bauhof, 352 Church Lane, Philadelphia, Pa. 19144

Figure 12–7: Practice rooms should be designed for many uses and should be equipped for conducting a variety of activities

planned to house the choir, band, orchestra, small instrumental groups, and listening classes. Theory and harmony classes, which are usually smaller than the mass activities, can also meet in this room. The size of this all-purpose facility, again, will depend upon the largest number of students who will use it at one time. If the choir of 90 voices is the largest music group in the school, and we allow 20 square feet per student, a minimum of 1,800 square feet will be needed. The height of the ceiling, preferably, should be about 15 feet. Allowance should be made for proper soundproofing and ventilation. Adjacent to the one large classroom, space should be available for the storage of instruments, choir and band uniforms, music, recordings, and tapes, and for office space and practice rooms. Care should be taken, also, to allow room for expansion as the program grows.

A wide program can exist within these limited facilities, but it will take much organization and planning. A small program will enlist the services of a smaller staff. A plan which involves only two teachers will reduce the number of activities which can be scheduled. This staff will have to develop a variety of skills which will make them versatile enough to meet growing and changing needs. There are many fine programs existing in schools with a minimum of space for the music department. If teacher skills are not limited and are flexible, much can be done to overcome the limitations of space. Furthermore, a going organization can only blossom out in an ever growing program which will take advantage of the built-in room for expansion.

Preparing the General Music Classroom

Where there is an extended music suite it is desirable to have a general music room. This classroom, whenever possible, should have an atmosphere of intimacy. The objectives of the class make it desirable that the class size be reduced to a maximum of 28 or 30 students. This renders the large choral or instrumental room impractical unless one corner of the rehearsal area is used. If a separate general music room is planned it should be no smaller than 30 by 35 feet, and it should include facilities and equipment necessary for conducting the class. Ideally, it will be an all-purpose room. Classes in music appreciation, music literature, theory and harmony, and creative music can be scheduled in it. This is the classroom where three or four pianos can be placed in order to conduct piano classes. A fine stereo tapedeck and record player should be included in the equipment which is planned. Adequate blackboards and bulletin boards should be provided on all sides of the room where student work and current newspaper and magazine clippings can be posted. In formulating specifications, special consideration should be given for soundproofing, proper lighting, and ventilation.

Planning the Music Department Office

Some elaborate facilities include a private music director's office. This, however, will tend to isolate the director from the program. It is desirable for a central place to be planned where all teachers can meet, examine reference materials, and pick up music recordings and other classroom trappings which are currently being used. A large music department office can include the desk of the director. All other teacher desks can be placed in classrooms. The central location of the office should include materials used in common, stored in cabinets or in shelves, either in the office or in storage rooms adjacent to the office. There should be a rack or an all-purpose table which will serve as a place for sorting music. Phonograph records, tapes, instrumental and choral music, charts, pictures, displays, books, and pamphlets should be sorted, indexed, catalogued, and made available for teachers to use on short notice. These should be stored in the office or in a room easily accessible to the office. Student librarians can be trained to assist in keeping the index files up to date. In this way, the music department office and the library of teaching materials become the central facility in the department.

Storing Music and Books

Teachers who are busy have little time to waste in looking for mislaid materials. A system must be devised which will facilitate the storage and filing of music materials. One of the best ways to file choral music, for example, is to use choral music filing boxes, which can sit on shelves. The title of each, name of the composer, number of copies available, and the index number can be recorded on the outer rim. There are several different types of commercial boxes which can be purchased. Some are more durable than others, but all can be used to good advantage. Once the system is organized it should not be too difficult to maintain. The choral music library should be filed in the music department office or in an adjoining room. Instrumental music is more easily filed in folders which can be indexed and stored in legal size, metal filing cabinets. This may also be placed in the music department office or in an adjoining storage room. Music text books can be stored in storage rooms or closets close by. They are not used as frequently and can be taken out for assignment to students early in the year or brought out as needed for reference work or as a part of classroom teaching. Here, again, the importance of availability and proximity must be stressed.

Planning Storage Space

Music, books, choir robes, jackets, stoles, band uniforms, hats, shakos, flags, musical instruments, orchestra jackets—all require areas of storage space. In planning a new music department, it might be best to locate these storage rooms between the rehearsal rooms. These additional air spaces can provide a soundproofing pocket between the choral and orchestral rooms. Often, the storage rooms can be used for additional purposes: (1) Part of each room can be set aside for a listening facility, where record players with earphones could be provided. (2) Some space can be set aside for the repair of reeds and musical instruments.

The walls of one of these storage areas should be lined with cabinets and lockers for the storage of instruments. Of necessity, storage bins must be custom built by carpenters to meet special needs. In some of the larger instrumental rooms, big instruments are stored along one wall of the classroom where students have easy access to them at rehearsal time. Where space is available it is probably best to store the instruments in the large instrumental practice rooms. If these closets reduce the size of the classroom, and thereby limit it, most of the smaller instruments should be stored in an adjoining room. In setting up these storage areas, provisions should be made for proper ventilation and adequate temperature controls. Excessive moisture damages musical instruments which have felt pads or wooden and glued sections. Correct storage is required. Proper locks should be placed on all cabinets and doors to insure against theft and vandalism.

The size of the instrumental storage room, of course, will depend upon the amount of equipment to be stored. Planning for expansion is wise, since it becomes difficult to find storage space once a music department facility is completed. The floor space should have a minimum area of 25 by 25 feet. If the ceiling can be placed high, windows can be located high on one of the walls above the storage cabinets. Several of the walls could have storage bins up to the ceiling to provide space for instruments and equipment which are not used regularly. In some schools, the instrumental storage room takes the shape of a long corridor where both sides are lined with storage bins, each one labeled and marked with the name of the instrument or the name of the student who plays it. Some of the instruments are owned by the school; others have been purchased for students by their parents. Sufficient space should be provided to store instruments when they are not in use.

In most schools, audio-visual equipment is handled by a special department and shared by the entire school. A large metropolitan high school, however, will require many projectors, screens, and record players. These are sometimes assigned throughout the school by departments. The music department, therefore, usually ends up with a complete set of visual and aural aids to be stored and used as needed by the department. This equipment can include motion picture equipment, filmstrip projectors, slide projectors, a radio, a television set, the opaque projector, sound tape recorders, and video tape recorders. In addition, there are usually other types of aids such as the stroboscope, tuning bars, metronomes, pictures of musical instruments, posters, charts, bulletin boards, display cases, a library of films, slides, records, and tapes. Modern music education requires the use of the most recently developed materials and equipment. These aids add a new dimension to a well-organized program. Space will be needed to store the materials and equipment.

The music educator should be familiar with the various visual and aural aids which enhance his teaching. Simple operations such as the replacement of a projector lamp or the splicing of torn sound tape should be learned in order to save hours of waiting for a technical assistant or repairman to arrive. The scientific, artistic, and mechanical know-how of the music teacher is important in that it helps with the teaching of the pupils. Facilities, equipment, and materials have significance only in that they become devices used by the teacher to make learning more meaningful.

Building the Music Department Library

The music department library is an essential part of the facilities available to students for research and growth. The collection of materials encompasses more than a collection of books to be found in the school library. Included here are reference books; novels and biographies of musicians; books which deal with musicology, theory, harmony, and creative music; books about musical instruments; books that deal with the relationships of music with science, the arts, history, and related subjects. Copies of many of these books can be placed in the school library for reference. The music department library, however, must be methodically and purposefully built and filed for immediate use in the department facilities. This includes choral and instrumental scores, instrumental and vocal instruction books, opera scores, symphonic skeleton and complete scores, solo selections for instrumental and vocal classes, chamber music for smaller instrumental ensembles, and a variety of miscellaneous material.

The library should also include recordings which are used in the classroom. A teacher can collect for the music program recordings of all of the significant symphonies, concertos, overtures, chamber music works, operas, art songs, folk songs, and popular songs, as well as recordings to be used with social studies classes and foreign language, English, art, and science classes. The collection may grow in size to well over a thousand albums. Adding definitive recordings, music dealing with the Renaissance, the Baroque period, the Classical and Romantic periods, the Post-Romantic period and the Modern period, we find that the accumulated materials require a large amount of storage space and a cross-indexed file system which will permit the teacher and student librarians to find needed recordings on short notice. The addition of stereo sound tapes to the library broadens the dimension for presenting sound recording at its best. Music teachers are now turning to tapes which have selections measured off in foot-lengths and can be conveniently used in the classroom. Storage of these materials becomes an important factor in the utilization of space.

We have tried to present a number of problems involved in planning for the organization of facilities, equipment, and materials in a new music department. The successful completion of plans and the implementation of facilities will depend upon the amount of money available for constructing a new plant; the knowledge and experience of the architect, engineers, and consultants; and upon the utilization of practical suggestions of music educators who are familiar with the needs of the music department. If the plans provide opportunities for the continuing expansion and flexibility of the program, the philosophy which underlies any good music education program will be reflected throughout the entire school.

Index

A

Academic music program, 23
Aptitude:
    for an instrument, 73
    for music, 32
Assemblies, 28, 133–151
    audience participation, 136–130
    committees, 134–135
    community singing, 137–142
    in general education, 135
    function of music in, 133–136
    music programs, 143–151
    scheduling, 135, 170

B

Band, 62–67
    community relations, 64
    concerts, 65
    marching, 25, 62
    musical growth, 66–67
    repertory, 65
    scheduling, 169–175
    seating charts, 66–67, 68–70
    stage and dance, 82
    tuning, 66

C

Cantatas, 164
Carnegie Units, 179–180
Changing voice, 39–40, 49
Choir, concert and a cappella, 25, 40–41
    morale, 48
    musicianship, 89
    rehearsal problems, 44–48
    repertory, 49
    scheduling, 169
    seating, 43–44
    sightreading, 43
    tone quality, 41
Classroom management, 185–189
Communication, the language of music,
        37
    with administration, 25
    with community, 23, 54
    with parents, 23
    with school board, 192–193
Community relations:
    and the band, 64
    and the choir, 49
    and the teacher, 192
Computer:
    and the integrated curriculum, 20

Computer: (*cont.*)
  and scheduling, 175
Concerts, 153–159
Contemporary music, 94–96, 191
Contests, 165
Courses of study:
  choral, 40–43, 49
  general music, 28, 32–37
  instrumental, 58, 61–62
  music appreciation, 98–112
  organic curriculum, 116–130
  theory and harmony, 92–95
  voice classes, 50–53
Creative music:
  scheduling, 169
  theory, harmony and composition,
    92–96
Credit, 179–181

D

Demonstrating and teaching:
  contemporary music, 191
  general music classes, 32–38
  instrumental music, 61–62, 65–66,
    73–76
  new skills, 20
  organic approach, 115–131
  part singing, 43
  popular music, 54
  specialties, 20
  taste and discrimination, 20, 32
  tone quality, 41
  voice classes, 51–52
Developmental approach, 102
Discipline, 47, 55
  at the band rehearsal, 65–66
  at the choral rehearsal, 44–48
  at the orchestral rehearsal, 77, 81

E

Electives, 21, 32, 51
Electronic equipment, 20, 32, 41, 112,
  120, 191, 207, 212, 213–214
Equipment:
  auditorium, 199–201
  classrooms, 202–212
  electronic, 20, 32, 41, 112, 120, 191,
    207, 212, 213–214
  lighting, 204
  musical, 207
  practice rooms, 209
  risers, 204, 207
Ethnic music, use of, 20, 35, 54
Evaluation:
  by the student, 37
  by the teacher, 37

F

Festivals, 159–161
  seating arrangements, 158–161
Folk music, use of, 20, 35, 54

G

General music, 7–9, 22–23, 25–26,
  27–38, 49–50
  approaches, 32–38
  balanced content, 35–36
  exploring in music, 36
  function of, 26, 31
  in general education, 7, 21–23, 27–28,
    115–116, 161, 175
  logical approach, 32
  preparation for specialties, 28
  program development, 30
  psychological approach, 32
  scheduling, 169
  technics, 87–92

H

Harmony:
  creative approach, 92–96
  modern, 94
  scheduling, 169, 178
  units of work, 92–94
Homework assignments, 189
Honor points, 181
Humanities, 20–21

I

Instrumental instruction, 57–84
  brass, 58
  elementary school, 58–60
  groupings, 58–59
  group technics, 59–65
  guitar, 54
  junior high school, 58–61
  percussion, 58
  repertory, 65
  scheduling, 169
  senior high school, 58
  small ensembles, 58–61, 169
  strings, 58, 75
  technics, 72–76
  woodwinds, 58
Instrument making, 33
Integrated music program, 7–8, 23,
  25–26, 27–28, 40–41, 49–51, 66–67
Integrating subject matter, 167, 175, 183,
  115–131
Interpreting music, 84–86
Introduction to instruments, 32
Involving students, 22, 154

L

Library, music materials:
  band, 65, 213–215
  books, 213–215
  choral, 48–49, 213–245
  instrumental, 61, 213–245
  musicological, 213–245
  recordings, 113, 243–245
Listening opportunities, 112-113
  radio, recordings, television, films, 163

M

Marching band, 25, 62
Motivation:
  for general education, 115–116
  for instrument playing, 59–60, 68–72
  for the marching band, 62–63
  for the orchestra, 68–72, 76–77
  for singing, 39–40
Music appreciation, 98–112
  aptitude, 32
  assemblies, 28, 133–151
  through choral singing, 40, 43, 49
  clubs 169
  contemporary music, 94–96, 191
  curriculum, 28, 49–50, 96, 166, 182
  through festivals, 159, 161
  folk and ethnic material, 20, 35, 54, 100
  in the harmony class, 29, 92–96
  by teaching interpretation, 84–86
  in instrumental activities, 58, 61–62
  library materials, 61, 65, 113, 109–111, 169, 176
  in the music literature class, 97–113
  in the theory class, 29, 92–96, 169, 178
Music as an elective, 20–21
Musical comedy, 162–163
Musical growth, 30, 32–35, 37–38, 39–40, 49, 52, 54, 58–61, 66–67, 82–83
Musicality, 85–96
Musical response, 86–89
Musical revue, 163
Music, and art, 20–21, 118–119, 129–130
  and the concerns of youth, 19, 22–23, 122–126
  and creative work, 30, 85–96
  and credit, 96
  and the dance, 130, 163
  and dramatics, 163
  and educational goals, 20, 22–23
  and English, 115, 126–129
  and foreign language, 33–34, 115, 119, 125–126
  and the handicapped child, 178–179
  and mathematics, 115
  and quality education, 22

  and physical education, 118–119, 135, 163
  and science, 115, 119–120, 136
  and the social studies, 34–35, 115, 120–125, 135
Music appreciation:
  course of study, 109
  developmental approach, 102–104
  emotional approach, 98–102
  form, 107–110
  intellectual approach, 98–102
  other listening opportunities, 112–113
  psychological approach, 111–112
  scheduling, 169
Music clubs, 169
Music curriculum, 28, 49–50, 96, 166, 182
Music education for competent amateurs, 23
Music facilities, 196–216
  all purpose rooms, 198–199
  auditorium, 199–201
  band room, 207–209
  choral rooms, 204–207
  ceiling level, 202
  classrooms, 202–207
  department office, 212–213
  general music room, 212
  lighting, 202
  location, 198, 201–202
  orchestra room, 207–209
  practice rooms, 209
  small music department, 209–211
  storage space, 213–215
  teacher involvement in planning, 196–199
Musicianship, 20, 23, 27–28, 43, 45–47, 51–53, 54, 84–96
  in the band, 66–67
  in choral groups, 89–90
  in the dance band, 82, 96
  dictation, 92
  eartraining, 92
  flatting, 87–89
  form and analysis, 92, 102, 107–109
  listening, 92
  rhythmic drills, 92
  sight singing, 92
Music in a changing world, 19
Music in general education, 25, 27, 38, 115–131, 151
  curriculum, 22, 116–119, 166
  objectives, 27
Music in the school budget, 8, 198–199, 209, 197–216
Music specialties, 7–8, 23, 24–25, 27–28
  band, 29, 62–67
  choral groups, 29, 40–50
  dance and stage band, 82
  general music for, 23, 28

Music specialties (*cont.*)
   instrumental classes, 29, 58–62
   opera workshop, 29, 161–162
   orchestra, 68–82
   organ, 29
   piano, 29
   theory and creative work, 85–96
   voice classes, 29, 51–54

N

Notereading, 37, 43

O

Opera Workshop, 29, 52, 161–162, 169
   materials, 52, 161–162
   scheduling, 169
Operettas, 162–163
Oratorio, 164–165
Orchestra, 68–82
   balance, 76
   concertmaster, 76
   first chair position, 76
   intonation, 76
   repertory, 81–82
   scheduling, 169
   seating, 76–80
   technics, 65–66, 73–76
   tuning, 75
Organ, 29
Organic curriculum, 116–119, 182
   creative work, 29, 85–96
   the dance, 130, 135–136, 163–164
   dramatics, 162–163
   English, 115, 126–129
   foreign languages, 33–34, 115,
      118–119, 125–126
   home economics, 136
   mathematics, 119–120
   music and art, 21, 118–119, 129–130
   physical education, 118–119, 135, 163
   science, 115–120, 136
   the social studies, 115–119, 120–125,
      135

P

Performance:
   by choral groups, 40–41, 49, 149–151,
      155–156, 159–162, 164–165
   by combined groups, 149–151, 159–165
   by instrumental groups, 57–58, 62–65,
      81–83
   in the community, 154–159
   in school, 153–165
Piano instruction, 29
Popular music, 20, 33–35, 53–54, 95–96,
   97–98, 100

Practice rooms, 59, 179, 209
   equipment, 179, 209
   scheduling, 179
Problems in music education, 19–26, 58
Professional organizations, 193

Q

Quality in music education, 22, 27–28, 32,
   34, 36, 38, 41–43, 46–47, 55, 58,
   62–67, 71–76, 81–83, 84–96

R

Recruiting:
   instrumental program, 71–72
   school orchestra, 71
   specialties, 31–32, 49
   strings, 71–72
Rehearsal room:
   all-purpose, 198
   auditorium, 199–201
   band room, 66–70, 207–211
   choral room, 43–46, 202–207
   orchestra room, 76–80, 207, 211
Rehearsals:
   band, 65–66, 74
      seating charts, 66–70
      sectional practice, 66–70
      tuning, 66
   choral groups, 44–48
      morale, 47–49
      musicianship, 43
      seating plans, 43–46
      sight reading, 43
      tone quality, 41
   orchestra, 68–82
      balance, 76
      intonation, 74–76
      seating plans, 76–80
      setting up, 66, 77, 79
      singing tone, 73
      strings, fingering, 75
      tuning guide, 74
Relevancy in music education, 32–36,
   94–96, 191
Repertory:
   band, 65
   choral, 48–49
   orchestra, 81–82
   theatre, 53–54
   voice, 51–54
Responsiveness to music, 85–92
Rhythmic training, 44, 92

S

Scheduling, 167–181
   computer, 175

Scheduling (*cont.*)
 conflicts, 20–23, 168
 the disadvantaged child, 178–179
 duplication, 24–26
 flexibility, 168–169
 the handicapped child, 178
 instrumental classes, 61–62
 interrelated activities, 28–29
 practice rooms, 179
 teachers, 23–24, 170–175
Shepherd's pipes, 33, 71
Skeleton scores, 103
Staff development, 183–195
Staff relationships, 191
Student, committees, 48, 134, 135, 154
 evaluation, 37
 interest, 30
 morale, 36, 43, 48, 55
 needs, 38, 50–51, 109, 111–112
 talent, 31, 49–50, 53, 71, 89–90
Support for the music program, 22, 24–26
Symphony orchestra, 82

T

Talent:
 encouraging, 30–31
 scheduling, 178
Teacher:
 assignments, 23–24, 194–195

classroom management, 185–189
communication, 189
and the community, 192–193
development, 183–195
and disciplines, 185
flexibility, 20, 55, 168
and homework, 189
morale, 24, 193–195
personality, 184–185
and professional organizations, 193
qualifications, 23–24, 182–185
resourcefulness, 191
schedule, 23–24, 166
selection, 23–24
skills, 23–24, 30
and staff relationships, 191–192
training, 23–24
versatility, 20, 54–55
workload, 23–24

V

Variety show, 163
Vocal music program, 39–55
Voice classes, 29, 51–53, 89–90
 repertory, 52
 scheduling, 169
Voice production, 29, 51–53, 89–90
 in assemblies, 139
 in vocal ensembles, 41, 44–47, 53–54